Husband
SCHOOL

Husband SCHOOL

WHERE MEN LEARN THE SECRETS OF MAKING WIVES HAPPY

Julie N. Gordon & David E. Gordon

Other books by Julie N. Gordon

BOOK ONE

Wife School:
Where Women Learn the Secrets of Making Husbands Happy

BOOK TWO

Skinny School:
Where Women Learn the Secrets to Finally Get Thin Forever

BOOK THREE

Happy School:
Where Women Learn the Secrets to Ovecome Discouragement and Worry

---

Live with your wife in an understanding way.

—1 Peter 3:7

If you are well read and biblically mature, please read this first.

We would like to warn you that this is *not* a biblical exegesis on marriage. There are some excellent ones, such as *Recovering Biblical Manhood and Womanhood* by John Piper and *The Meaning of Marriage* by Tim Keller. This is merely a practical book to help husbands decode the mind of their wives.

A husband is called to love his wife in order to reflect a picture of the heavenly Bridegroom's love for his Bride, *not to manipulate her to serve him.* Again and again, the wisdom character in this book says, "Focus on how you love, not on how you're loved and given to." Our immature protagonist, Jason, does not understand this call at first, so please be patient with him.

Please know that similar to the way the authors of *Charlotte's Web, The Velveteen Rabbit,* and *The Lion, the Witch, and the Wardrobe* used toys and animals to speak profound truths, we have used a genie to convey wisdom in this story.

And last, note that *Husband School's* protagonist may appear a little crass in places, but he is a student with much to learn.

Dedication

To Stephen, Joseph, Jonathan, Benjamin, Samuel, and Trent

Our prayer is that you love your wives with the sacrificial and servant heart of Jesus.

Table of Contents

INTRODUCTION

Understand That You Are the Gardener

Monday, September 17

At two o'clock today, my financial future will be altered forever. Charles Bateman and I are meeting to finalize our partnership to build my unique line of gyms all over the South. For ten years, I have worked toward this moment, this spectacular, almost intoxicating moment. Today is the day I begin my life as co-owner of a dynasty.

By permanently transforming *not only* the bodies but the minds of my many multimillionaire clients in Dallas, I've proven I have something different to offer the world of fitness. Now I'm ready to build my empire of gyms, so I can revolutionize the physiques and minds of not only the affluent but also the average Dick and Jane. The genius in my method is that as a personal trainer, I teach my clients how to achieve the mental discipline necessary to accomplish their goals. Teaching others how to acquire this disciplined thinking is my gift to the world. My gift just needs some greenbacks, hence my two o'clock meeting with Charles Bateman.

Since my regular noon client is out of town, I decide to swing home and shower before the uber-important two o'clock meeting. Excitement as well as nervousness is pulsating through my body.

Walking into our kitchen, my wife Christina is in her slouchy sweat pants, holding Samantha, our baby. Samantha is crying, and Christina is trying to clean up some peanut butter splattered on the floor. Three-year-old Mason is hanging onto her, whining that he wants to go outside. Our five-year-old, Isabella, is absent from this zoo because she just started kindergarten. Christina has no makeup on, the kitchen is a total mess, and toys are flung all over the hearth room.

Ignoring the chaos, I jump right in with my excitement. "My two o'clock meeting today with Charles Bateman may be the turning point of my life," I say. I wait for Christina to express her wild enthusiasm and praise for my entrepreneurial spirit.

"Don't get your hopes up too high, Jason," she warns. Immediately, she turns to Mason and speaks to him irritably.

Handing me Samantha, who has peanut butter smeared on her shirt, Christina adds, "It is a risk for someone like Charles Bateman to invest in you, Jason, since you've never run a large business. I wouldn't be surprised if this doesn't work out," she says solemnly.

The frustration I feel at her lack of support is beyond description. When we got married seven years ago, I thought I was marrying a beautiful, encouraging woman who would be my constant cheerleader as well as a constant excitement in the bedroom. Boy, was I wrong, especially about the bedroom part.

"Can't you ever support me, Christina?" I say as I deposit the baby into a nearby playpen. I turn to walk toward the bedroom so I can shower. Although I am scared about building my line of gyms, at least I have some confidence that I can learn to do it. I have zero confidence, however, for this pathetic marriage.

"I try to be realistic," she calls after me, "and then you get offended. I could use a little support, too, by the way."

Undressing to shower, I realize how sick I am of this marriage. I'm sick of her mouth, and I'm sick of her sexual frigidity. In every other area of my life, I'm great. My clients love my charming personality, I'm good-looking, my friends laugh at my jokes, and when I'm interested in something, I'm not lazy. And if that's not enough, I know more than anyone how to change one's mind-set, so they can get permanently fit and lean. My life is terrific with the exception of this exasperating and disappointing woman who shares my bed.

I remember that later today I train Delaney Rutherford, the twenty-six-year-old daughter of one of my richest clients, Thomas Rutherford. I feel guilty that I look forward to her training sessions. In contrast to Christina, Delaney is always in a good mood and always encouraging. I bet I can count on her to be excited when I tell her about my co-ownership in my new life-transforming gyms.

After showering, I still have an hour before the birth of my empire, so I drive to my own gym/office, a large room that I've furnished with weight training equipment. Actually, the space is a trade with one of my baby boomer clients, Kevin White, in exchange for personal training. Normally the rent would be at least $1500 a month, but Kevin says the space is a thank you for helping him shed fifty pounds and for permanently changing his mindset about food.

Entering my gym, I notice a package outside the door. Picking it up, I bring it inside. It is addressed to Mr. Jason York. That's strange. I don't remember ordering anything.

Opening the package, I discover a mahogany box. Proceeding to open the box, I find an old brass lamp inside with a handle and a spout. It looks like it belonged to Aladdin. Is this some kind of lame joke? Who would send me this junk?

Picking up the lamp, I notice there is a cork in the spout. Maybe the joker who sent this left a note inside the lantern. Removing the cork from the spout, I see a plume of smoke arise. Immediately, I'm startled. Dropping the lamp on a chair, I move into the hall to escape what I fear is going to be an explosion. When there is no explosion, I peek back around the corner.

Standing in my office is a dark, middle-aged Middle Eastern man. He is about six feet tall and is built like the Rock, Dwayne Johnson. His tanned skin looks a little dry, like a man who has played tennis all his life without sunscreen. He is wearing gold silk pants that are topped with a white embroidered vest, and he has a large turban on his head.

Seeing me, he motions for me to come to him. "Do not be alarmed, Young Jason. I am your Genie, and I am here to grant you one wish."

What nonsense is this? Am I having a dream? I slap my thigh, but I don't wake up.

"It is true," he continues. "I am your Genie, and I am here to grant you one wish, Young Jason. What is your wish?"

How does he know my name? Who is this? My heart is racing, but his calm eyes tell me not to be alarmed. Slowly, I move toward him. Realizing that if this is a dream, I will eventually wake up, so I decide to play along with his shenanigans. Thoughts of my cold, critical wife and our repeated conflicts come to mind. Coming up with the right wish is an easy choice.

"Okay, Genie, my one wish is this: I want an outrageously happy marriage!"

"Your wish is my command, Young Jason. Would you like to begin the lessons now?"

"Wa—wait a second," I say. "Begin wh—what lessons? Can't you just say 'abracadabra' and make my marriage wonderful?"

"Of course I can, Young Jason. But you would still have the same behaviors, attitudes, and thoughts, and in a matter of weeks, you'd be right back where you are today. This is not a short term solution. I'm going to enroll you in my *Husband School*. I will teach you how to understand your wife, how to meet her needs, what will win her heart and affection, and *how to love her in a language she can hear*. When you master these timeless secrets, your wife will turn toward you with great affection and a new desire to meet your needs."

"Me? I'm going to learn to understand *her*? How to love *her*? Why not make her understand and love *me*?" This genie obviously doesn't get that this is a man's world.

"When you master these secrets and principles," he says, "your wife will respond and reciprocate with warmth and devotion."

Warmth? Devotion? Obviously, this dude doesn't have a clue how mentally unstable and emotionally dysfunctional Christina is.

"Men feel like women are an endless pit of knots and tangles, but actually, there are only eleven principles that a man needs to know in order to love his wife in a fashion that delights her. Understanding these eleven secrets is not an overwhelming task but merely a minor learning project. You understand football, you know how to work a smart phone, and you know how to sculpt the human body. You can learn these principles and master the art of marriage."

"You are comparing things I like—football, iPhones, and my body—to something I don't like—my marriage. I didn't have to try to learn those subjects; they came to me easily, as if by osmosis."

"Yes, you're correct that most men are not interested in taking the time to learn the precepts that create a fantastic marriage. But *the quality of your marriage dictates a large portion of your happiness,* so I suggest you learn these secrets."[1]

This is total malarkey.

"At the beginning of marriage, a man understands that he is to love his wife," the Genie says. "And men are happy to give their new wife 'love.' But soon, a husband realizes that what he believes is love—such as bringing home his paycheck, being faithful, having sex, and sharing activities together (without talking about or working on the relationship) is *not* making his new wife happy. This new husband has no idea what his wife wants, but whatever it is, *he knows he's not giving it.*"

"I did love Christina when we first got married. But now, she's never satisfied, constantly wanting more from me. Honestly, I'm not even sure what she wants."

"Marriage is not an unpredictable, chaotic situation," he says. "There are patterns and skills in marriage that promote harmony, friendship, and

---

1. A healthy and loving marriage is a picture of the Gospel (Eph. 5:32).

affection, just as there are patterns and behaviors in marriage that produce discord, conflict, and a gulf between spouses. Learning the patterns and skills is not rocket science."

"Why aren't you addressing her?" I ask. "My wish was for a warm, happy marriage, and it looks like I'm the one being asked to change. She's the problem." Stick that in your emerald turban.

"Women are responders,"[2] he says. "It is a rare situation when a woman does *not* respond to a husband who gives his wife these eleven relationship principles."

"I'm sorry, Genie, but I'm not buying into this. I'm not the problem. You see, she's a bit of a crazy. She's hysterical, critical, and unreasonable. By the way, her mother is also mentally off, so I think Christina got her genes."

The Genie is laughing. "I cannot tell you how many husbands in my *Husband School* have said the same thing. Christina is not mentally unbalanced. She is merely responding to a husband who does not *understand*[3] her. Because she feels frustrated, she frequently escalates in anger. What you are calling *crazy* is merely a woman who feels misunderstood and unloved. Just give this a chance, Young Jason. When your wife feels cherished, safe, and cared for, she will become like a prize rose garden on a queen's estate."

Sure, but all I'll get will be thorns and thistles.

"Think of Christina right now as an untended garden," the Genie says. "Her soil does not have the right nutrients, the bugs are devouring her flowers, she is not getting adequate sunlight or water, and weeds are growing everywhere. I will teach you to be a master gardener—in your marriage. Then you will watch your wife, as a well-tended garden, bloom and bear much fruit. By the time you have implemented all of my eleven lessons, Christina will respond to you as if she is altogether another woman."

---

2. We are not trying to say women are helpless and passive. Nevertheless, most women respond positively to the eleven principles in *Husband School*. Please note that if either of you is struggling with abuse, addiction, or adultery, please see a Christian counselor.

3. This whole book is about understanding your wife, because it is definitely not programmed into your DNA. "Live with your wife in an understanding way" (1 Pet. 3:7).

I'm wishing I could rewind and not have married Christina, but instead, he wants me to learn some dumb secrets about tending a garden. The only garden I'm interested in is Madison Square Garden, where there is going to be some extraordinary basketball played in a few months.

"Men are simple creatures,"[4] he continues. "This simple nature the Creator designed enables a man to focus in an intense fashion on his calling. A woman, by contrast, is multi-dimensional.[5] The Creator designed her to be complicated, with her many simultaneous responsibilities of childcare, food preparation, and home management, not to mention a job of her own. Most men can only acknowledge *what they themselves experience*, and since men can't experience a woman's perspective, they tend to deny its existence."

Surely they would sell books on ESPN to teach men this stuff, if it were true.

"If a man gets enough sex and does not experience too much emotional turmoil in the marriage, then he is usually satisfied. But it takes much more to satisfy a woman's complex nature—but not an infinite amount."

This is pitiful and worthless information. He keeps insinuating that maybe I'm not doing something right. The fact is that I married the female version of Darth Vader.

"Okay, Genie, fine, if women are a little different. I can handle that. But Christina is in a category of her own. No matter what I do, it is never enough."

"Men like to say that 'no matter what they give, it is never enough,'" he explains, "but that's not true. When a garden is given the proper amount of sunlight and nutrients, it blooms every time. The same is true of a wife."

"Let's say I give these eleven secrets a chance," I say. "When do I get to tell Christina what I want and how she should change?" After all, that's what I'm really interested in.

---

4. By *simple*, we only mean that men are generally simple in comparison with women. This stereotype seems to hold true with the couples we have worked with around 80 percent of the time.

5. Proverbs 31 delineates the plethora of responsibilities for the noble wife.

"After you consistently take care of your garden with these eleven ingredients, your wife will turn to you, open to you, and be able to hear you. She will then be receptive to working on what is important to you. Right now, however, she cannot hear you. You, the gardener, must first tend your garden. Until you consistently deposit these eleven nutrients, you are not to ask her to change. Agreed?"

"Okay," I say aloud, but in my mind, I know that if she really hits one of my buttons, I'm not sure I'll keep this promise. A man can only take so much from a woman.

"Young Jason, before you married, you worked to win Christina. But now, you act as though the work is done. Can you imagine planting a garden in March and then not looking at it again until fall, yet expecting a bountiful harvest? You have the wrong mind-set. A garden does not grow beautiful and lush unless you tend it regularly and properly."

This is a terrible analogy. A wife should take care of herself, take care of my ego, be a faithful assistant, be an engaging companion, take care of my sex drive, and do it all cheerfully.

"Most men naturally think about thirty percent work, thirty percent money, thirty percent sex, and ten percent for everything else," he says. "A woman, on the other hand, thinks about numerous and diverse topics, such as how her relationships are going, whether her house is clean, whether the children need haircuts, and how things are going at her job. She wonders if the curtains match the color scheme of her living room and if there is enough healthy food to eat in the house. In addition, she cares about how she looks, whether the house is freshly painted, and whether her husband will expect sex tonight. She cares about the temperature in the room, the kids' costumes for Halloween, decorating for Christmas, her girlfriends, her weight, your dirty fingernails, and your fast driving. And all these topics and many more are always pulsating through her mind."

What a drag to live with a female brain.

"Therefore, a man cannot trust his natural inclinations on how to love his wife well, not only because she occupies so little of his thoughts but also because he does not understand her complex nature."

Work, money, and sex are not the only things I think about. There's my golf game and football, just to name a couple other important subjects.

"I understand what you want from your marriage, Young Jason. You want her to praise you, appreciate all that you give her, respect you, let you lead without resistance, assist you, adapt to you, be attractive, warm, affectionate, laugh easy, be interested in everything about you, be a good cook, take care of your children, and meet your needs in the bedroom."

"Yes, *that list* is exactly what I signed up for," I blurt out. This guy is reading my mind.

"But there's an order, and the order is that you learn first to meet her needs, and then slowly, ask her to meet yours. You can't storm through life, demanding that she shapes up and gets with the program. If you want that kind of life, join the Marines."

The Few. The Proud. I always thought that slogan described me.

"A husband's tendency is to see what he is *not* being given," he says, "such as respect, credit, praise, appreciation, sex, and a willingness to adapt and follow. But a humble husband must lay down these demands and first focus on meeting the needs and desires of his wife. It is only after she feels loved, known, and cherished that she will turn to him and be open to pleasing him."

Christina trying to please me? Yeah, that's a nice wish, like shooting par at Pebble Beach.

"Do not be deceived by the long-held belief that no man can understand the mind of a woman," he says. "That is now known to be absolutely false. The minds of women have been dissected, analyzed, and categorized. What she wants is not impossible to discover or difficult to understand. The challenge for a man is to give his wife something *he doesn't understand, want, or think is necessary.*"

This is nauseating.

"As you know, there are rules in life. There are rules of gravity that apply when one jumps from a building. There are rules for good health, such as not smoking or overeating. There are rules that no matter how loudly you protest, you cannot change. This is how it is with women. There are rules about how you must treat them, if you want them to be happy in a marriage. You can shout that the rules are ridiculous, or you can concede to what has been true for centuries. You will not escape the rules written in the DNA of women, however clever and powerful you might be."

Clever, yes. Not so powerful...yet!

"Mankind has learned over the course of centuries that for a man to fully enjoy and experience life, *he desires a warm relationship with a woman with whom to share it*. Instinctively, men know this. Therefore, a wise man makes a choice to learn how to make this creature happy or else he will suffer being alone, either physically when she leaves, or emotionally because she cuts him off."

Christina hasn't left physically, but she has certainly left emotionally.

"I'm leaving now, as I have a massage in Istanbul. When I return after your two o'clock meeting today, I will begin my specific instructions, so your wife will feel loved, understood, and cherished," he says as he dissolves into a whirlwind of smoke.

With only fifteen minutes until my critical meeting, I think about the Genie's talk. What bunk it all was. Christina will never change, no matter what nutrients I give her so-called garden. The thought of being saddled to her for the rest of my life startles me momentarily.

Pulling into the parking lot of the impressive and prestigious high-rise office complex owned by Charles Bateman, I put the Genie's tirade out of my mind. Glancing around, I realize that right now I am merely a personal trainer with a dream. But in a few minutes, when I walk back out of that building, I will be the co-owner of a regime. Taking a deep breath, I enter the building.

SUMMARY

Understand That You Are the Gardener

Do...

> . . . know that marriage is not an unpredictable, chaotic situation. You can learn the patterns and skills to promote harmony, friendship, and affection.

> . . . know that when a woman consistently receives the eleven *Husband School* tenets, she will turn to you and be interested in your happiness because women are responders.

> . . . view yourself as the gardener who must supply what his garden needs. A woman does not have the same needs you have.

> . . . know there are rules about how you must treat a woman if you want her to be happy in your marriage.

Don't...

> . . . expect your garden to bloom without much attention and care.

> . . . assume that the mind of a woman is unknowable. The mind of a woman has been dissected, analyzed, and categorized. It is not impossible or difficult to understand.

LESSON 1

Understand Your Wife's Desire for Deep Conversation

Still Monday, September 17

Walking into Charles Bateman's intimidating high-rise, I think back to when this dream of building my phenomenal line of gyms was born. During my first two years of college, I mistakenly mainly partied. Having torn my ACL during my senior year in high school, I had quit exercising. When one of my fraternity brothers volunteered me to play Santa Claus at the upcoming Christmas party, it was a wake-up call.

That insulting remark made me realize I had gained thirty flabby pounds since the golden days of my junior year in high school when I was the point guard and MVP of the basketball team. The day after the Santa suggestion, I got back in the gym. Researching weight loss, I discovered that "eating clean" transforms your metabolism. And the best information I discovered—the most important ingredient in fitness—is how to acquire the mind-set and mental discipline *to postpone what you want now for what you want most.* In six months, I transformed my flab into sculpted muscle.

Meeting with a business school professor over coffee during my junior year of college to discuss my career plans, I first shared my love of fitness. After that discussion, he asked if I knew what I wanted to do specifically for a career. When I told him my plans to climb the corporate ladder, he commented, "Really? When you were talking about fitness, you were ablaze with energy. But the moment you started talking about the corporate ladder, you went lifeless. Are you sure that's what you want to do?"

For two months, I couldn't get the professor's words out of my mind. I had always thought I would work my way up in a large business. I mean, that's what my father wanted me to do. But this conversation made me realize I wasn't excited about that prospect. What I was sincerely pumped about was transforming people's lives with weightlifting, nutrition, and teaching them to be mentally tough. So I changed my major to exercise physiology.

When I told my dad about my new major, he exploded. "That's a wimpy major. You should have consulted me." I guess my dad's dreams of reading about me in the *Wall Street Journal* as some hotshot CEO were vanquished. But that was his dream, not mine.

In no time, I had set a goal to build three gyms by the time I was thirty and to own fifteen facilities by the time I was forty. Not merely gyms with equipment, but gyms that alter thought as well as triceps.

Being thirty-one now, I'm behind schedule in building even that first gym, but that's okay. It took longer than I thought to get a master's in nutrition, to get certified as a personal trainer, and to become certified as a weight loss coach. Getting married and having the stork drop three babies at our house in the last five years hasn't helped me reach any financial goals either. I am now ready, however, to offer my secrets to the world. I just need Charles Bateman's money.

Entering the conference room, Charles Bateman is seated at a large, gold-gilded conference table where expensive, European-looking paintings flank the walls. Charles is accompanied by a team of dark suits. Standing up to greet me, Charles offers me a seat next to his. His suit probably cost a couple thousand dollars. I decide my Joseph A. Banks suit, which I bought at a Buy One-Get Three sale looks adequate.

"Welcome, Jason," Charles begins. "Men, this is the young man I've been telling you about, Jason York," and he introduces me to all the

Brooks Brothers around the table. I expected to have some casual conversation to break the ice, but Charles seems focused on getting started with our meeting.

"We have reviewed your proposal carefully and are ready to discuss the details of our business arrangement," he begins. My heart pounds with excitement. Charles first defers to his accountant and attorney, who talk about venture capital, accumulated depreciation, and asset turnover. Much of this is over my head. I ask a few questions and nod to pretend I understand perfectly. I know everything about carbohydrates and muscle fatigue, but little about debt financing and acquisition costs.

After all the men speak, Charles smiles at me and says, "For your ownership portion, Jason, we would like to offer you ten percent."

Did I hear him correctly? What did he say? Ten percent? I am bringing the innovation, and I am doing the work, while he is doing nothing but fronting the money? Maybe he's talking about ten percent of something else.

"Uhh, Charles, what do you mean exactly, ten percent?" I ask politely.

"I mean I would own ninety percent, and you would own ten percent. You'll get a salary Jason, and of course, there will be bonuses along the way; that is, if profits exceed our projections."

"Charles, I…I'm the one who has the knowledge to change people's lives, and I…I'm the one doing the work," I stammer.

"Yes, my boy, but I'm the one with the cash." His wingmen laugh. Sweat breaks out under my collar.

"I wasn't ready for that kind of split," I say. The henchmen look down.

Gathering his papers on the table, Charles replies, "Why don't you think about it, Jason? Then we can meet again to discuss it further, if you'd like."

Without any more conversation, the meeting is officially over and all of Bateman's yes-men suddenly ignore me, talking among themselves, like I'm only here to clean up the refreshments. Stunned, I pick up my worn briefcase to exit.

Frustration builds in every part of my brain. Charles Bateman wants me to build a dynasty of my one-of-a-kind, life transforming gyms, and then he gets ninety percent of the profits. My starched shirt makes it difficult to breathe. I feel like I did when I got cut from the eighth grade football team because I was too small.

Glancing to my right, I am momentarily alarmed by the sudden appearance of the Genie in my front seat. "That was a disappointing offer, Young Jason," the Genie begins, as if he had been with me all afternoon. Feeling devastated from the meeting, I'm definitely not in the mood to listen to this joker again. But since I don't know how to ditch him, I guess I'll have to.

"We will now begin our discussion of the eleven principles that you need to know in order to take exquisite care of your garden," he begins. "The first principle is Understand Your Wife's Desire for Deep Conversation."

Deep conversation? How boring is that?

"Young Jason, you understand that you want Sexual Release regularly, right?"

Wanting it and getting it are two different things. "Of course," I say.

"With the same intensity, your wife also wants a Release regularly. But for her, it is an Emotional Release, gained when she has Deep Conversation. Since you have little or no need for this release and don't understand it, you think it doesn't justifiably exist, or you believe it is a dysfunctional quality in women."

Emotional Release? Sounds like a virus that could destroy mankind. "Genie, I've never even heard of Emotional Release."

"Men feel close by having Sexual Release, but women feel close by having Emotional Release," he says.

Real men don't do this.

"Not having Deep Conversation with your wife feels to her like indifference and neglect," he says. "Affairs are not as much about sex as they are about a desire to feel important, a desire for attention, and a desire to feel known. Remember, your wife is your garden and Deep Conversation is like sunlight to your garden."

Women should have a sign on their foreheads before marriage that reads, "Warning: Marriage may be hazardous to your health."

"Since men have not been schooled in the art of understanding women, they are quick to debate this statement. But generations of women show it's true. *Women want talk, and men want sex.* And giving women what they want makes them open to giving you what you want."

Is he hinting that I might get more sex if I gave more talk?

"I am going to teach you how to have soul-stirring Deep Conversation with your wife by dividing the topic into three aspects," he says. "The three aspects are World Class Listening, Initiating Conversations of Significance, and Taking the Shield Off Your Heart."

Seriously? He's going to break down the topic of *talking*?

"The first segment is to give your wife World Class Listening," he begins.

"Ehhh, excuse me, Genie, but you're going to teach me how to *listen?*" But immediately after saying that, I remember when Christina was talking recently about her mother's upcoming birthday party and instead of listening, my mind had wandered to my new Callaway wedges. Christina had said, "Jason, you're not listening."

Another memory surfaces of the time and expense I spent last year, when I planned a surprise birthday party for Christina. Afterward she had said, "I've told you I don't like surprise birthday parties. Besides, I told you I wanted a new sofa for my birthday. You don't listen to me, Jason."

"The way to give World Class Listening," he says, "is to Hit the Ping Pong Ball Back."

My ping pong backhand in college was amazing. Our fraternity ping pong team, of which I was a stellar member, was placed second in the annual Greek Ping Pong tournament. Now *that's* an interesting subject.

"When Christina begins a topic," he says, "ask her a question or make a comment that allows her to go even deeper into the subject. For example, if she begins to tell you the story about how upset she is that her girlfriends didn't include her in their weekend getaway, you *don't* Hit the Ping Pong Ball Back when you say, 'That's crazy. They should have invited you. What's for dinner?'"

Uhhh, I cut Christina's stories short all the time, because otherwise, they would go on for eternity.

"Instead, Hit the Ping Pong Ball Back, so she can more fully express her feelings on the topic. For example, you could say, 'What do you think they were thinking?'"

"Genie! No! That would only encourage her to continue!" I'm not doing this junk.

"It doesn't matter if her subject matter is interesting to you," he says. "Quit wasting time and energy thinking about that. *This is the woman you were given to love.*"[6]

I can't do this. I don't *want* to do this.

"If you listen briefly, disagree or argue, criticize her, or yawn—versus listening deeply to understand—you get zero points. Sure, after you have carefully listened and want to offer other options, that's fine. But most men jump in with answers before their wife has finished talking and felt understood."

One time when Christina was going on and on about how she felt about her involvement in the PTA at Isabella's school, I said, "Can you scroll to the end?" She broke down in tears and ran to the bedroom. Another time during one of her long, detailed stories about her anti-aging skincare program, I interrupted and said, "Just give me the bottom line, okay?" She stood up, glared at me, and stomped off.

"This level of listening takes time and energy," he says, "and since men have no desire or need for this level of sharing, they resist it. Untrained husbands want to have sex, get a sandwich, and then watch ESPN highlights."

Right on. Men rock.

Christina's topics bore me to the ends of the earth. Here I am, a man

---

6. "Husbands, love your wives, just as Christ loved the church and gave himself up for her" (Eph. 5:25).

with huge, important goals, and my wife wants to talk about how Isabella needs some tennis shoes like the other little girls in her kindergarten class. Or worse, she wants to discuss whether I think she should cut her hair. I should not have to be burdened with her frivolous topics. If Christina talked about Dustin Johnson or Jordan Speith, I could give World Class Listening.

"Christina would never be finished talking," I argue. "Never."

"Admittedly, the amount of conversation that women desire feels burdensome to men. However, when I teach *Wife School* to women, they tell me they don't *want* to have sex with their husbands as often as their husbands desire it. I teach women that willingness, not arousal or desire, is the first step in sex. The same is true for you with giving Christina World Class Listening. Willingness is the first step, not desire."

This is preposterous hogwash.

"The second aspect to having Deep Conversation with your wife is to Initiate Conversations of Significance. No wife is ever richly satisfied in her marriage without sharing deep topics, such as her fears and her dreams. Therefore, you have to learn to be a master at asking questions about significant topics, such as, 'How do you feel about my parents? How do you feel about our church? What do you think about our family's involvement in our community? How do you feel about our money? What's on your mind? What's important to you right now?' These conversations, if you will have them, will put you in a unique league of husbands. A wife longs to discuss her deep feelings, but most know that her husband is not interested."

No normal male wants to hear this rubbish.

"This one *Husband School* principle widely separates husbands because men are reluctant to give something they don't want themselves," he explains.

I wonder if he's making this up.

"Men will do anything to avoid giving their garden this important first nutrient of Deep Conversation that women desperately want," he says. "To express their love and faithfulness, men would rather buy things for their wife, take care of the yard, or build a bookcase. While all these gestures are appreciated, they are no substitute for giving your wife these two aspects of Deep Conversation: World Class Listening and Initiating Conversations of Significance."

If the other ten secrets are as ridiculous as this one, I'm dropping out of *Husband School.*

"She doesn't deserve this," I say adamantly.

"No wife deserves this,[7] but that's not the point. The point is, this is how you love your wife in a language she can hear, and it's your duty and responsibility to love her."

It's her duty to have sex with me, but apparently, she didn't get the memo.

"A woman who does not feel listened to, understood, or explored will begin to close her heart to you," he says. "She may give you sex or do your laundry, but it will only be out of duty."

Men rule the world. Why should any man put up with this?

"In the whole world, there is little more attractive to a woman than a man who draws her out and understands her heart. With this kind of treatment, a wife turns toward her husband and begins to open her heart to what her husband wants."

Sure. And I've just won the Clearinghouse Sweepstakes.

"If a husband repeatedly Initiates Significant Conversation and then listens deeply, he will eventually understand his wife's top concerns, goals, and dreams. When you give yourself to knowing and understanding your wife deeply, it melts her heart like a microwave melts ice."

This advice is extremely annoying because in contrast, I believe a wife should be an assistant, a concubine, a housekeeper, and a nanny, regardless of the class of my listening.

"It would be impossible to ever understand Christina," I say, thinking she probably has some diagnosis related to female schizophrenia.

---

7. "The heart is deceitful above all things and beyond cure. Who can understand it?" (Jer. 17:9).

"This is said by men who won't make the effort to search and discover what is in a woman's heart," the Genie replies. "If men work diligently to read their wife's heart, they will find that she indeed can be understood and known. However, because Christina does not feel known, explored, and understood by you, she does not want to be affectionate, admiring, or have frequent sex with you," he says.

"That's ridiculous!" I almost shout. "Anyhow, she should go first. If she gave me more sex and praise, I might try to listen better."

"Men think women talk too much, and women think men want too much sex," he says. "The natural inclination is to give what one *wants,* so men are eager to give sex and women are eager to give conversation. But wise gardeners are not governed by *their* needs—gardeners are guided by their garden's needs."

There's got to be a better way to get Christina to give me what I want.

"The third segment to mastering Deep Conversation is to Take the Shield Off Your Heart," he says. "It can be quite burdensome to men to articulate how they feel and what is going on with them at a deep level, but a woman wants to tell you everything she's thinking as well as to hear everything you're thinking."

She wouldn't like some of my thoughts about her.

"I try to talk to her, and then she isn't interested," I say.

"Maybe she's not interested in your rec basketball accomplishments or your Fantasy Football statistics, but I can promise she's interested in your hopes, dreams, regrets, and goals."

I don't even think much about that junk, so how am I supposed to talk about it?

"Try to spend at least twenty to thirty minutes a day giving your wife Deep Conversation by giving her World Class Listening, Initiating Conversations of Significance, and Taking the Shield Off Your Heart," he says. "This conversational time each day turns marriage in a new direction."

I have trouble finding time to work out as it is, and this nitwit wants me to talk to my wife twenty to thirty minutes a day.

"For some men, it is easier to give Deep Conversation throughout the day. Have a little talk in the morning about her upcoming day and how she feels about it. Call her during lunchtime to see how her day is going. Ask questions, and listen well. Have a time every night where the two of you talk. Both spouses should know the other one's current and long-term goals, dreams, concerns, regrets, and disappointments."

Hearing this makes my stomach feel like I might have a mild case of food poisoning.

"Genie, if Christina and I talk more, she will only use the opportunity to unload her machine-gun criticism on me. She gets on me for everything. She doesn't like how I drive, what shoes I wear out to dinner with her friends, or how I talk to the kids. It's like she thinks I'm a moron and she's the mother who is supposed to correct me."

"Women do have a long list of what they care about," he admits. "After you have given Christina these eleven non-negotiable tenets of *Husband School,* she will turn to you, and you can ask her for what you want. But for now, try to overlook her offenses."[8]

Sorting paper clips all day sounds better than this assignment.

"I am leaving now to visit my tailor in Thailand, but I will return," and with a twirl of smoke, he is gone.

That was ridiculous and untrue information. This numbskull wants me to spend a lot of time and energy listening intently to Christina. Not gonna happen, Bud. The other idiot thing he said was that giving Christina Deep Conversation will give her Emotional Release, and that is equal to my desire for Sexual Release. That's bunk, too. I refuse to buy into this nonsense.

Thinking that Christina will never change makes me feel trapped. I love the children, but the antagonism of the marriage makes me wish I could dump it all, run away, and start over.

Again, the disappointment of Charles Bateman's offer reenters my mind. What a rotten day.

---

8. "A person's wisdom yields patience; it is to one's glory to overlook an offense" (Prov. 19:11).

Pulling into the parking lot of Thomas Rutherford's office at 4:00 p.m., however, I feel a new surge of energy as I remember who I am training at 4:00 p.m.—Rutherford's twenty-six-year-old single daughter, Delaney. I train most of my clients at my gym, but Rutherford has a full weight room created just for his convenience, so I meet Rutherford and his daughter here to train. I'm relatively certain he pays for his daughter's personal training sessions, as most twenty-six-year-olds can't afford me. Honestly, I would drop my prices if necessary, so I could continue to train her.

"Hi, Jason," she says, her eyes beaming. She is on the treadmill, warming up for our session. I think her outfit is new, as I don't remember seeing it before. Her extremely short, hot pink workout shorts firmly grab her well-toned thighs, and her top exposes her tiny waist as well as her bulging breasts. It's a little too much to take in. That familiar surge in my body tries to overtake me, but I push it down. Delaney's beauty and sex appeal drive me crazy.

Keeping it professional, I take her through a vigorous workout but struggle the entire time not to notice her buttocks and breasts. It's more than a normal man can handle. After the session, we chat about local restaurants, a couple recent movies, and her eyes reveal she finds me attractive. Leaving her father's gym together, I feel overcome with all my sexual craziness that has no legitimate outlet since my wife is about as affectionate as the Statue of Liberty.

Walking into the kitchen when I arrive home, I realize that staying overtime talking to Delaney has made me late.

Christina is again holding the baby, Samantha, in her left hand and stirring something on the stove with her other. Mason, the three-year-old, is jumping up and down on the sofa in his dirty shoes. Isabella, our five-year-old, is twirling around the kitchen in her ballet outfit. "Daddy, you're late. Tonight is my ballet class!"

Christina doesn't even look at me.

"I'm sorry—I was finishing up a session with a client," I explain.

Christina still doesn't look at me, and now the baby is crying.

"Let me change clothes first," I say, discouraged, and I begin to walk toward the bedroom. Christina doesn't ask about the meeting with Charles Bateman, and it's just as well because I would just have to listen to "I told you so."

"There's no time for changing clothes," she barks, like a sergeant giving orders. "It's time to take Isabella."

Christina turns back around to keep stirring, and I notice her buttocks from the back. Maybe Christina would agree to some sex tonight. It's been more than two weeks.

"Okay, I'll be ready in five minutes." Lowering my voice, I say to her, "What do you say about, you know, tonight, when I get home, after we get the kids in bed?" My body is ablaze with desire.

Christina quickly turns around and with an icy cold glare out of her eyes, snaps, "I'm not really in the mood, Jason. Anyhow, I was hoping you would watch the kids when you get back from your ballet run, so I could get out of here a couple hours and have a little time to myself to do some shopping."

Shopping? As in spending money? Money on what? Shoes? Purses? How many of those things does a woman need? Before the arrival of our first baby, Christina worked full-time as a dental hygienist. But after our first baby, Isabella, was born, she dropped to a mere twenty hours a week, so I have carried the brunt of the financial load. Every day, I feel like Atlas with the weight of the world on my back.

"How long will you be gone?" I ask.

"These are your kids, too, you know, and I need a break. Geesh, I ask for a little time out, and you come unglued."

"I'm not unglued, Christina. I only want to know how long you want me to watch the kids."

I get no sex, my credit card is going to the mall, and now I'm a babysitter. What kind of concentration camp am I in? I guess now would not be a good time to ask for a sandwich for the road.

"No one helps me around here, and I'd like a little free time, too," she says as she stomps off to the bedroom.

How did this happen? Somebody please tell me. How did our marriage get like this? Christina is a dang rope around my neck, always complaining, always wanting something more from me. It's exhausting and unrelenting. I'm pretty sure that idiot Genie guy has never tried to fix a marriage as messed up as mine.

Waiting on Isabella's ballet class to finish, I simmer. This is not the marriage I wanted. That buffoon talked about giving Christina some World Class Listening, but how do you listen to a dragon spewing fire?

Hearing my text message beep, I glance at my phone. It's from Delaney. "Great workout, today. I can feel all my muscles tingling. Can't wait until next time!"

As I feel the pleasure from reading her text, I also feel the guilt, knowing I should find pleasure instead from my wife, not from another woman. I'm discouraged about finding funding for my new business venture, but even more, I'm sick about having said vows to a woman whom I don't like.

SUMMARY OF LESSON 1

Understand Your Wife's Desire for Deep Conversation

Do...

... realize that not having Deep Conversation with your wife feels like indifference and neglect to her.

... realize that a woman's soul aches for her husband to give her World Class Listening and who will Hit the Ping Pong Ball Back.

... know that women are delighted when you Initiate Conversations of Significance.

... know that your wife wants to be known, explored, and understood by you.

... take the Shield Off Your Heart and share your hopes, dreams, regrets, and goals.

Don't...

... treat her as she deserves. Instead, give your garden what it needs.

... assume your wife should want sex like you do, but realize most wives want *talk* (Emotional Release) to the extent that you want *sex* (Sexual Release).

LESSON 2

Understand Your Wife's Desire for Admiration and Appreciation

Tuesday, September 18

Christina is trying to get Isabella ready for school, control rambunctious Mason, and feed the baby in the high chair. Thankfully, I get to escape this jungle. Booking early training appointments is specifically for this reason.

"Your mother texted me yesterday," Christina says, "and wants to come visit, Jason." Although I'm ready to leave, I think about the Genie's lesson on Deep Conversation, so I decide to give it a try.

Leaning against the breakfast bar, I ask, "Really? How do you feel about my mother coming to visit?" I'm even surprised to hear myself say those words.

Christina looks up from feeding the baby to read my expression. My mother's long visits have been the topic of many uncomfortable discussions. Since my mother lives in Seattle, and it is expensive to fly to our home in Dallas, I think she should be able to stay a week. Repeatedly, Christina complains about the length of her visit and wants her to stay only three nights. Telling my mother what I want her to do has never been easy, as she is used to getting her own way.

"You know how I feel," she retorts. "I'm happy for your mother to come three nights, but anything over that exhausts me. I can barely keep up with the kids and the house, and then when your mom comes to town, she expects me to drop everything and entertain her." She looks back down, ready for the same old argument.

"She really tires you that much? And you're already exhausted with the kids and the house?" She has said this a million times, but now that I'm really trying to listen, I decide to explore this.

Her expression flattens. "Yes, I'm exhausted, Jason, and your mother's long visits throw me over the edge."

The sadness in her eyes is obvious. However, the thought of confronting my mother horrifies me. I'd rather wrestle a gorilla.

"You know how I feel about confronting my mother," I say.

"Yes, I know," she says, with even more dejection, like she's been running a marathon and doesn't have the strength to take one more step.

"Of course, I'm reluctant to confront her unless it's absolutely necessary. But I see that you're already tired, and you don't want a long visit from my mother. So, I'll talk to her," I say. What I'm going to say to my mother is a whole other story. She is not going to like being told how long she can stay.

Christina's eyes rise to meet mine, and there's the tiniest bit of thankfulness. It's the most peaceful face I've seen on Christina in months. "I would appreciate that so much, Jason."

I fear I'm making one woman happy at the expense of turning another into a cyclone.

"What will you say?" she asks.

"I guess I'll tell her the truth, that you're exhausted, and you only want her to stay three nights."

Christina's eyes flare, and I see the anger I know so well. "No, you can't blame it on me! That's not what I want. I want you to tell her that our household is busy right now, that we are barely making it, and therefore *you* don't think it's best for her to stay longer than three nights. I don't want to be mentioned!"

Good grief. I listen, I'm willing to confront my mother's strong will, and now I'm not saying the exact right thing. This Genie has never dealt with anyone as difficult as Christina.

"I try to listen to you, Christina, but it's never right or enough," I say as I move toward the garage door.

"I do appreciate you telling your mom to stay only three nights," she says as she follows me to the door, "but why do you have to blame me? Why can't you act like you're the one making the decision? Why can't you protect me?"

I drive off. What a hopeless marriage this is! The woman is impossible. Before I'm even out of the neighborhood, Christina texts me, "Remember tonight is Bunko and I need to leave at five-thirty."

I text back, "That's going to be tight because I have a late afternoon appointment." I train Delaney again today at four, and I don't like to be rushed.

"I can't be late. I'm a co-hostess tonight," she texts back.

Shaking my head, I burn with anger. Christina will never be satisfied. This Genie doesn't have a course to calm a rattlesnake, and that's what I need.

The day unfolds as usual, with my clients repeatedly thanking me for the life change I've given them by teaching them how to get their mind in the right place, which then gives them the self-discipline to eat clean and sculpt their bodies. My favorite appointment, Delaney, is next. Unwittingly, my energy rises, but I feel guilty for being excited.

Walking into her father's gym, Delaney is doing jumping jacks to warm up. I don't think she's wearing a bra, the way everything is bouncing around.

Challenging Delaney, I give her what I know is an exceptional workout. Her long brown hair is flopping around in a ponytail. Her tight, lean legs and butt are driving me mad. After our session, we chat a little as she towels off. Then the goddess-looking woman powders her perfect nose and applies some reddish-pink lipstick as we chat.

Locking up the building, we exit together. Delaney drives a yellow Porsche Boxster, obviously a gift from her father, as no ordinary twenty-six-year-old could afford a car like that. Delaney works for her dad, so maybe this is a company car. We say goodbye, and I get in my eight-year-old Tahoe. It doesn't start.

Immediately I text Delaney and ask her if she can come back, so I can use her car to jump my battery. She's back in a minute. Getting my jumper cables out of my trunk, we work together to hook up our batteries. At one point, she is trying to untangle the cables without looking where she is going, and she bumps right into me, head on. Her top assets drive right into my chest. My body again explodes with desire.

Thanking her, I get into my car to drive home, knowing I'll never make Christina's five-thirty deadline. In this traffic, it's at least thirty minutes to our house. Pulling out of the parking lot, I nearly wreck as the Genie again suddenly appears in my passenger seat. Just like last time, I'm not in the mood to talk about my marriage, but I do have a thirty minute drive, so I may as well listen.

"Genie, I tried giving Christina Deep Conversation, but she was unreasonable."

"Not to worry," the Genie says. "It will take a few weeks, if not a few months, to turn your marriage around. There are some deep habits and patterns that need to be replaced. Just stay at the helm, and the ocean liner of your marriage will eventually begin to turn around."

Promises, promises.

"The topic today is Understand Your Wife's Desire for Admiration and Appreciation," he begins. "This secret pulls your wife's heart to you like a magnet attracts iron, so you are wise to master this principle."

"Genie, I don't think you understand what's going on with Christina. I mean, there is very little to admire and appreciate about her." This might be a good secret for many husbands, but Christina is an unusual case.

"Many people believe one should not overindulge other people with too much Admiration and Appreciation in order to keep them in their place, or so they won't get the big head," he says.

My mother was afraid that we would get conceited, so she was usually quick to point out our weaknesses while largely ignoring our strengths.

"But this is false thinking," he says. "Most spouses feel under-encouraged and underappreciated. In fact, if a husband begins to daily admire and appreciate his wife, this alone will substantially alter the climate of a marriage."

Probably an exaggeration, but I'll let it go.

"This kid-glove treatment of your wife is again, something you give to her, not because she deserves it, but because you decide to do what is right, and that means giving your spouse what she wants and needs to function at a high level. You give your garden the nutrients that make it robustly bloom."

At least he agrees she doesn't deserve it.

"Intentionally thinking about Christina's virtues, gifts, and abilities—and then *commenting on them*—is a powerful secret that quickly and powerfully turns Christina toward you," he says.

Christina takes my good looks, hard work ethic, and great wit for granted, but nobody cares about that.

"Wives will never be fully satisfied and fulfilled in marriage, Young Jason, unless they live in an atmosphere saturated with Admiration and Appreciation. A husband can be average in many areas, such as personality and earning ability but can become a world class husband in his wife's opinion, when he learns how to make his wife feel valued, beautiful, talented, and special by giving her large doses of daily Admiration and Appreciation."

I would be content with a small dose of Admiration and Appreciation.

"Men underestimate the cry of his wife's soul to be reminded daily about her positive qualities, actions, and talents. Every day, every single day, your wife wants to hear what she does right."

And they say *men* have big egos.

"Genie, she treats me like I'm some villain, yet I'm supposed to give her this Admiration and Appreciation garbage? How do you suppose I could ever be motivated to do that?" I still think he should find a way to get Christina to change and then ask me to do this.

"A husband does not give his wife what she *deserves*," he says. "A wise husband gives his wife what she needs and wants, instead of demanding what he needs and wants. Later in *Husband School*, after you learn and implement the eleven non-negotiable secrets to making your garden bountiful, Christina will be a completely different person, and she will be interested in giving you what makes you happy."

He must really think I'm naïve to fall for this foolishness.

"First, we will discuss the specifics of Admiration," he says. "After you have been to a brunch in which omelets are served, it is an opportunity for you to say the omelet was good, but Christina's omelets are still the very best you've ever had. After Christina organizes the neighborhood Halloween event, tell her what fun and creativity she adds to your family as well as the community. When you consistently have socks and underwear in your drawer, tell her that her attention to detail is a gift to all those she's around."

"Genie, are you sure Christina wants to be praised about putting socks and underwear in my drawer?" This is pretty ridiculous.

"Wives, like gardens, get dry, and Admiration is like water. Wives enjoy Admiration about everything. If she works as an interior decorator, tell her how her beautiful designs give her clients peace and beauty in their homes. You want to find all the positive you can about your wife and then sincerely comment on it. If you look for opportunities to praise her, you'll find them everywhere. These words make a woman feel happy in her marriage, and the absence of them makes her feel alone and sad."

Let me buy her something. Let me fix something for her. Give me something else to do.

"Diametrically opposed to giving your wife Admiration," the Genie says, "is bragging on other women. Never say, 'Angela is what I call a great cook!' or 'Did you see how clean Kelly's house was?' And certainly don't say, 'Emily sure kept her figure in spite of all her pregnancies.'"

Uh, I said that last week about a girlfriend of hers, hoping Christina would start ditching refined carbs and sugar and work on regaining her pre-kid figure.

"You must be on the lookout for areas to compliment: her looks, her personality, her mothering, her creativity, her character, her management of the home, her involvement in the community, her performance at her work, and the countless other activities she engages in. Giving Christina Admiration will incredibly delight her and quantumly increase her happiness in your marriage."

But what about *me?* No one is trying to delight me.

"The opposite of Admiration is criticism," the Genie says. "Criticism is like a stampede of wild horses tromping through her garden."[9]

Critical remarks I've said to Christina over the years come back to me: "Guess you got busy and overcooked the roast, huh?" Another time I told Christina, "I'm a breast man," even though Christina's breasts are small. She told me later that made her uncomfortable undressing in front of me. And then, there's the memory of her obsessing over what to wear to a wedding, and she cried when I said, "It doesn't matter what you wear to this wedding because no one looks at women over thirty."

"Now, let's turn our attention to Appreciation," he says. "To begin appreciating your wife, start noticing what benefits you receive from her and comment on them daily," he says.

"Genie, is *daily* really necessary?" I say as I'm certain he overdoes these teachings.

"Mother Teresa said that there is more hunger for love and appreciation in this world than for bread. People are starved for appreciation. This is something, again, you choose to give your garden, so it will thrive."

"But what will I say? I'll run out of stuff to say after the first 'Thank you for cooking' and 'Thank you for doing the laundry.'"

"Young Jason, your wife's benefits to you are almost endless. Tell her

---

9. "Death and life are in the power of the tongue" (Prov. 18:21).

you appreciate her being a wonderful mother to your children, her good sense of humor, her honesty, her calm spirit that soothes you, her being organized with the household, her interest in the community, the way she takes care of herself, or how she makes sure you have healthy dinners every night. Notice some benefit she brings you every day. It is extremely rare in marriage that spouses appreciate each other enough."

I can vouch for that being true in my direction.

"Appreciate that she always let you know when she's going to be late. Appreciate that she does the lion's share of the childcare. Appreciate how much cooking she does. Appreciate how much fun she is and how much more you enjoy life because she makes you laugh."

Enjoy life more? Uh, that's almost the polar opposite from how I feel.

"If she is always in a good mood, appreciate that. If she presses through when she's tired, appreciate that. If she makes your lunch, takes care of you when you're sick, or has your family over to dinner, say a few special words of sincere Appreciation. There is no end to what a man will discover that his wife does right if he will pay attention."

And there's no end to what I do right, but who's counting?

"A husband wields huge power over his wife's self-esteem," he says, "and his daily words either build or destroy that self-esteem."

I didn't agree to this.

"Remember, treating your wife with these eleven *Husband School* tenets puts oxygen in her gasping body. It is water for your garden, and you are the gardener."

All I can do is sigh. The thought of gearing up to give Christina Deep Conversation and now, Admiration and Appreciation, is depressing as well as annoying.

"I know giving Admiration and Appreciation is overkill for you," he says, "but women need constant reassurance about their beauty, desirability, and gifts. No wife is ever truly fulfilled in her marriage unless there is Admiration and Appreciation for the duration of the entire marriage. Even if you're faithful, dutiful, and a good provider, she is not deeply satisfied unless she feels admired. This is not hard to do, once you are in the habit. I am going to Dubai for a mud body wrap, but I'll return for lesson three," and he swirls into a funnel of smoke.

The Genie keeps harping on this idea that I'm to focus on how I love and give, not on how I'm loved and given to. How does any normal man do this in my intolerable situation?

Walking into the kitchen from the garage, I'm fifteen minutes late because of my car trouble. Christina meets me as I walk in and hands me the baby. "I knew you'd be late," she says. Before I can explain about my battery, she says, "What's with the lipstick on your shoulder?"

Looking down, I see Delaney's pinkish-red lipstick on my white Under Armor workout shirt. She must have accidentally gotten it on my shirt when she bumped into me while we were untangling the jumper cables. "Can you explain that, Jason?" she asks.

Completely shocked, I begin to explain how Delaney helped me jump the car and must have gotten lipstick on me when we bumped into each other. "She has lipstick on after a workout?" she asks in disbelief.

She shuts the door in my face and leaves.

Who can believe this absurdity? As hot as Delaney is and as loyal (outwardly) as I've been—especially in the face of Christina's disrespect and lack of sex—and then to be falsely accused. How much can a man take?

Discouraged I walk into the den carrying Samantha. Mason just dumped his spaghetti on the floor and hit Isabella, who is now screaming. How did I get myself into this pandemonium? And the bare-chested sage wants me to give Christina not only Deep Conversation but also Admiration and Appreciation? My marriage sucks. That horrible D-word (*divorce*) comes to mind. I know better because I made a lifelong vow to this woman, but the truth is, I want out, and I see no lifeline out of this pit.

SUMMARY OF LESSON 2

Understand Your Wife's Desire for Admiration and Appreciation

Do...

. . . intentionally think about your wife's virtues, gifts, and abilities, and then comment on them (Admiration).

. . . realize that a wife wants to be reminded *daily* about her positive qualities, actions, and talents.

. . . realize that criticism is the opposite of Admiration.

. . . notice what benefits you receive from your wife and comment on them daily (Appreciation).

Don't...

. . . admire or brag on other women.

. . . think that if you're faithful, dutiful, and a good provider, then you are free from giving your wife this nonnegotiable tenet.

LESSON 3

Understand How Your Wife Feels about the Big Five

Saturday, September 22

Because I'm playing rec basketball this morning, my heart pumps a little faster than usual. This Saturday league is one of my favorite things in life. Not only are my lungs stronger than most of the other guys but I can still consistently swish a three-pointer. The twenty-year-old guys have respect for my athleticism, and being thirty-one, that feels good.

Getting up early, I make coffee, prepare my own breakfast, and head to the gym. On my drive there, I'm annoyed as I think about last night, when Christina and I went out with some of her girlfriends and their husbands. She knows I don't enjoy those bozos, but she insists on these outings anyway. The second we got back to the car after dinner, Christina started her stuff.

"Jason, I don't see why you can't try harder. I mean, you hardly said anything all night," she complained.

"I go out with you and your friends, and then because I'm not the life of the party, you're going to criticize me?" I asked incredulously. Tell me she's not doing this, I thought.

"You were like a bump on a log all night," she continued. "The only time you talked was when you were telling the table how many carbohydrates the chips had and how they screw up your metabolism. Don't you have any other topics?"

The anger I felt at her accusation cannot be described. I repeatedly feel that Christina doesn't appreciate anything I do, but instead, criticizes me for the tiniest fault. If only I could push rewind, I'd never get myself into this noose. But now—I'm saddled with three kids and a mortgage. I can't walk away, although I badly want to. Christina is not the girl I thought I was marrying.

Continuing my drive to my basketball game, I think back to when I met Christina in my college senior year. She was sitting in the cafeteria, all by herself, eating an apple and reading *Good to Great* by Jim Collins. I thought I'd never seen a girl so beautiful in my life. Her long, dark hair was twirled around and stuck into some concoction on top of her head. She had on a little makeup, some skinny jeans, and a long, tight-fitting tunic top. When she got up to get a refill on her drink, I got a good look at her long, lean lines from the back and decided right then I had to meet this girl.

So I mustered up the courage to walk over and ask her if she had some paper I could borrow as I just had an idea that I wanted to diagram before I forgot it. She smiled, as if she saw through what I was doing, and said, "So, you have some brilliant idea you don't want to forget? Tell me about it."

After telling Christina a little about my idea for my line of gyms, her eyes danced. "What an incredible concept that is!" And so began my infatuation with this creature. I decided I'd do anything to sleep with her, including marry her.

I did have to marry Christina to sleep with her. Soon after the wedding though, Christina started telling me that she didn't feel loved, that she didn't feel close, and that she didn't think we communicated deeply enough. On top of that, babies started showing up at our house. I'm still not sure when I agreed to all these children.

Sadly, I think about how things have changed, especially after we had kids. Now when I want to have sex, Christina always says another night would be better. In fact, Christina is now obsessed with the children, and I sometimes feel like an outsider in my own home.

Walking into the gym, I put all my unpleasant marriage thoughts on a shelf in my mind. Our game begins, and I am on fire this morning, just an absolute beast, as I hit all five of the three-point-shots I attempt in the first half.

My athletic prowess greatly annoys a player on the other team, a guy whose teammates call him Tower, obviously because of his six-foot-four stature and solid physique. Not only does Tower start playing dirty, throwing elbows and jabs, but he starts the trash talk. "Wow, Little Guy is having a moment. Let's see what we can do to stop Little Guy." He keeps calling me *Little Guy*, which I hate. Anyway, I'm five foot ten which is average, not little.

Tower begins guarding me too closely, and the refs must either be blind or lazy. Even with Tower's heckling and elbows, I still launch three more three-point-shots that go in, and we win. I wanted to say, "Take that, you Towering Punk," but of course, I didn't.

Driving home, my text message sound beeps. It's from Delaney. I stand outside on the driveway to read the message before I enter the house.

"Hey, Jason. I'm going out of town and need to cancel my sessions next week. But do you think you could have lunch with me a week from Monday to discuss some goals I have for my training? Could we meet at 12:30 p.m. at Modern Market?"

Caution lights flash and sirens sound in my head, but then I tell myself, "This is a client, and she wants to talk about her fitness goals. I also train her dad and two of his multi-millionaire friends. It would be a bad business decision to refuse her."

"Sure," I text back. "See you then."

A feeling of pleasure mixed with guilt descends upon me. Putting the feeling aside, I walk into the kitchen. Not only does Christina look like she is getting ready to personally implode but it looks like there's already been an explosion in the kitchen. Why can't Christina do a better job with her housekeeping?

Ignoring the mess and chaos, I announce, "I made eight three-point shots this morning in my game." I wait for her awed response.

"That's nice, Jason," she says without looking at me as she continues to unload the dishwasher.

That's it? "That's nice, Jason"? What about, "Oh, honey, you're an amazing man. Can you believe you can still outscore those young guys? You're awesome, Jason, simply a rock star of a man." That's what good wives say. I don't know why I still try to get blood out of this turnip. Deep Conversation and Admiration and Appreciation might be secrets that would make some wives feel loved, but nothing will work on this cadaver.

"I'm going to rake leaves in the backyard," I say. Anything to get out of the house. Maybe I should start training clients on Saturdays.

While changing into my yard clothes, Christina walks into the bedroom carrying a large basket of laundry to put up, ignoring me. I don't want to give her Admiration and Appreciation because she royally doesn't deserve it, but the Genie says I am to focus on *how I love and give*, not on *how I am loved and given to*. Dang, what can I lose? I'll try his Admiration bunk.

"Christina, I was thinking today about the time I met you."

Christina is putting up towels in the bathroom but walks to the door to look at me.

"You were?" she asks.

"I remembered how beautiful I thought you were, sitting there reading *Good to Great*, eating your apple." Should I tell her how hot she looked from behind or leave that part out?

Her face is suspicious. "Why were you thinking about when you first met me?"

Of course, I leave out the fact that she's now a huge disappointment from that first meeting, but I continue.

"I'm not sure why I was thinking about it, but I remember your hair was all twisted and put on top of your head, and I was just taken with your beauty. Then, when I told you about my dream of building a line of gyms, your face lit up. I thought you were intoxicating. I thought right then you might be The One."

How did I spit that out? I don't know. But regardless, delight is all over her face. She is embarrassed, as she is not used to hearing comments like this from me.

"Jason, uhhhh, well…that's very nice. Now, why are you telling me this?"

"Just because I thought it this morning." I leave out that a Genie told me to give Admiration even though she is as cold as Lake Michigan.

Christina smiles and leaves the room. She liked it. I can tell she did. She really liked it. As I walk out to rake leaves, I am somewhat encouraged.

Raking and burning leaves in the fire pit gives me a sense of satisfaction. What smells better than leaves burning on a sunny autumn afternoon? Surprisingly, the Genie shows up.

"What are you doing here?" I ask. "Christina is at home."

"No one can see or hear me except you, Young Jason," he says. "I am impressed that you moved toward Christina with Admiration. She obviously enjoyed your remarks."

"Maybe she did," I admit, "but she still treats me like I'm her employee."

"Young Jason, you have only had two lessons so far and there are eleven. You must be patient."

In my mind, I think of my three choices: (1) divorce her, (2) be miserable like I am now, or (3) give this loony guy a chance. I decide to go with door number three.

"Today we will discuss a topic that again surprises me because of how unaware men are of its power. It is called celebrating the Big Five."

"I have no idea what the Big Five are," I say, "but I know about the Big Twelve in college football, and the Texas Longhorns are looking good this year." He's not smiling. I guess genies aren't into college football.

"The Big Five occur every year for women," he explains. "The Big Five are her birthday, your anniversary, Christmas, Valentine's Day, and Mother's Day."

Oh, those stupid days, the ones which Hallmark has made a fortune of.

"Listen carefully, Young Jason, because since you feel radically different about our lesson today, your tendency will be to discount or ignore it."

Women and more of their sappy stuff. Is there no end to it?

"As untrue as it may be, women often measure how much other people care about them by *how others show up for them on their special holidays*. This is especially true concerning a woman and her husband. For a woman's special days, she wants a card (preferably mushy), a *wrapped* present, flowers, to be taken out to dinner, a cake (if it is her birthday), and a parade. Just kidding about the parade, but women do want each of the Big Five to be an *event*. If you don't roll out the red carpet on her Big Five days, you will pay, sir, as your wife will feel unloved."

I can't take this. I just can't. "Genie, I can't be a full-time husband. I'm a full-time personal trainer, and I'm trying to find funding for a line of gyms!"

"This is not very time-consuming after you get in the habit," he says. "You simply have to have your antenna up. Write her Big Five dates on your calendar. Every woman has a unique way she wants to celebrate her Big Five and this is one of the easiest ways to make your wife feel loved and cherished without that much work on your part."

It sounds like an enormous amount of work to me.

"A woman knows in her heart what she wants," he says. "If you get her a gift she *doesn't* want, she says to herself, 'He doesn't know or understand me.' And Young Jason, a woman will never feel cherished and loved if she thinks you don't know or understand her."

"When we first got married," I tell the Genie, "I asked Christina what she wanted for her birthday, and she said she couldn't think of anything. So I dropped it. And then, when we stayed home on her birthday, she came unglued, telling me how hurt she was. I mean, what nonsense! I had asked her!"

"You gave up too soon," he said. "You have to pursue a woman in this area. Gifts are huge to most women, as is appropriately celebrating the Big Five."

Irrational women with illogical thinking.

"Many women have a hard time asking for things, so you have to humbly suggest things," he says. "For example, you might ask her, 'Would you like me to buy us tickets to a play to celebrate our anniversary?' Or, 'Would you like me to make dinner plans for Valentine's Day?' A woman has a specific marriage playbook in her heart, and you have to extract it."

This Big Five thing is already making me mad.

"Offer suggestions to her, and she will let you know. Say, 'I was thinking that you might like me to surprise you with a trip. Would you like that?' Some women would love this, and some women would absolutely hate it. You must have a mindset that you will not be offended if she doesn't appreciate your efforts. Just keep offering ideas until you score."

This one secret alone is likely to reduce my nightly sleep from a measly seven hours to a paltry six.

"You could say, 'I thought you might like me to surprise you with a birthday party someday.' Some women will love this idea, and again, others will be mortified. Some will say, 'Well okay, if you only ask my two best friends.' *Don't surprise her unless you're relatively certain she will like your idea.* Men give what they *think* their wife wants and then miss it, and after all that trouble, they lose affection points from their wife because *they did not know her heart.*"

I barely have time to play golf now, yet he wants me to spend hours each week with this madness.

"If she's savvy with clothes," he says, "and you're not a clothes horse, then it's better if you say, 'I want to take you shopping and let you pick out a new outfit.' Or possibly, 'Do you want me to take you to pick out new lamps for your birthday?' If you suggest things, your wife will let you know, yay or nay."

No, I refuse to play this game.

"One husband said to his wife, 'I was thinking that you might like some perfume for Mother's Day. Would you like that?' His wife replied, 'Yes, I like Ciara perfume, but I only like 100 strength.' The husband came home with 80 strength, and the wife was annoyed because he had not carefully listened."

A husband buys the right perfume but gets the wrong strength, and his wife is disappointed? Women are impossible.

"Just be warned, Young Jason, the gift has to hit. If your wife is an avid runner, and you buy her running shoes from Walmart, you will get negative points as again, you missed her heart. You have to pay attention. Many men keep a list in their smartphone of things she mentions. But still, it is best to check it out instead of guessing. Ask your wife questions, secretly record her answers in your phone, and buy it later. It will make you seem like a thoughtful genius."

I'm a genius, all right, but I don't know about the thoughtful part.

"If gifts are not your thing," he says, "you can always buy her a mushy card, bring flowers, take her out to dinner, and then suggest taking her shopping to buy something she wants. There are very few women who don't adore this."

That was a four-step process he just mentioned: card, flowers, dinner, shopping. Waaayyyy too much work. And he wants me to do this five times a year? Insanity.

"Plus, if you want to really rock this area, in addition to showing up big time on her Big Five, you must deposit other Surprise and Unexpected Gifts (SUGs) each year."

Please, stop. My head is going to explode.

"We won't discuss SUGs any further, but know that she *expects* you to show up for the Big Five, so if you really want to delight and impress her, surprise her with a SUG *for no reason*. Again, this attention by you pays gigantic dividends."

"Does a man get anything else done in this world when he follows your *Husband School?*" I ask. "How does he have time to build his business when he's scratching his brain to stimulate Deep Conversation, give Admiration and Appreciation, and now, to celebrate the Big Five? What about hobbies? What about relaxation?" I'm starting to feel like a hamster on a wheel.

"It is indeed work, Young Jason, but work with a gargantuan payoff. Women adore being treated like this and will reward you with overflowing affection. This secret of celebrating the Big Five has an outrageous and colossal payoff."

Sex? Will this get me sex?

"If you suggest gifts, and she doesn't want them, do not label her unappreciative. Instead, tell yourself that you didn't do enough work to discover what was in her heart. If you probe, she will tell you what she wants."

No. No. I refuse to do this.

"Start asking her about her special days a couple of weeks, if not more, before the actual day. If you wait until a day or two before, it is very obvious to her that you don't really care."

Bingo. He got that one right.

"If you are the spender and she is the saver, though, she might not want a lavish outing or gift. You will have to talk to her. She might want a deposit in the orthodontist savings account or private-school tuition account. But she will have things she wants, like, 'buy gold for an investment,' or 'give the money to the church for missions.' There are things she wants. She has something she'd like to do with money: spend, save, invest, or give it away. Your job is to discover her heart."

Now, a great wife would want to save money so she could buy *me* some new Callaway irons. I deny myself all the time for the family, so wouldn't that make sense?

"Women are continually changing, so you have to repeatedly probe and explore to read her heart. To feel explored by a man is one of the most fabulous feelings in the universe to a woman."

All I get when I explore Christina are more ways she wants me to change.

"When you ignore the Big Five, Young Jason, your wife may not tell you, but there is a resentment she will feel toward you, as she says to herself, 'This is an opportunity for my husband to express love to me, and he didn't. Therefore, he doesn't really care about me.'"

"Absurd!" I retort. "A man just has other things on this mind!" I can't take this delusional female thinking.

"I will continue to explain to you *how a woman thinks and feels*," he says. "Women equate *how you treat them on the Big Five with how much you care about them*. It's just the way it is. You don't get to decide how women feel. You don't get to judge whether it is right or wrong. You only get to understand how they feel and then decide how you are going to respond. My advice is to understand how important the Big Five are to women, and then, to roll out the red carpet on those days."

"Genie, this sounds like a formula for a rich guy, and that's not me." Maybe I don't qualify for this baloney.

"For hardly any money on her special Big Five days, you can put her picture on the table, blow up balloons, make hand-written signs, fix her breakfast, and gather wild flowers. Most men find money to buy a new mountain bike or a new camera for themselves, but then say they don't have money to celebrate a wife's Big Five."

My $3000 John Deere riding lawnmower comes to mind. But that was a necessary purchase. The hydrostatic drive provides me with the speed choices that a man needs. And it saves me time to spend on more important things—like golf and televised football.

"Men repeatedly refuse to do the work to extract how a woman feels," he says. "But she is waiting to give you her love and devotion until she feels known. Not celebrating the Big Five in the specific manner she desires will make her feel unloved and unknown. Do the work, Young Jason, do the work."

The Genie disappears, and I seethe at these teachings. I am mistreated in my marriage, but yet I am to be some stupid gardener, revitalizing my garden. The Genie's whole mindset goes against everything I think. I'm the man. I thought she was the one who was to help me, and yet this buffoon continually asks me to not be concerned right now with *how she is treating me*, but to repeatedly focus on *how I treat her*. Just deplorable advice, that's all I know.

Christina sticks her head out the back door. "Would you please take Mason to get his haircut at one o'clock? That's when Samantha takes her nap, and I'd like to nap, too."

This is Saturday, my day off, and Christina has me doing her work. Surprise, surprise. Christina can't even take care of the three kids we have, yet she constantly pressures me to have a fourth. What a joke that is.

"The Longhorns play at one," I say. I can't be on call and start running Christina's errands. I mean, after all, this *is* football season. Men need to be free on weekends.

"There are games on all day," she says. "You will survive watching only five hours of football today instead of your usual six. I'll get Mason ready to go." She shuts the door without waiting to hear my response.

Really? How disrespectful is that? She can give me orders? I spit out all that romantic mumbo-jumbo and she gets to tell me what to do?[10] The Genie said to be sure and deposit all eleven secrets before I ask her for what I want, but the moment these eleven lessons are over, I'm going to tell her that I need her to quit bossing me around. It's humiliating and infuriating.

Angry and discouraged, I walk into the house and get in the shower. Again I think of how I tried to give Christina Admiration, and all it got me was missing the first half of Texas versus Alabama.

---

10. Of course, it is wrong for Christina to boss Jason around.

SUMMARY OF LESSON 3

Understand How Your Wife Feels about the Big Five

Do...

... realize that a wife often measures how much you care about her by how you show up for her on the Big Five.

... make each of the Big Five an event.

... realize that many women have a hard time asking for things, so you have to suggest ideas.

... realize that each woman has a playbook in her heart for how she wants to celebrate the Big Five, and you have to extract it.

... realize that she expects the Big Five, so if you really want to rock it, get her a SUG (Surprise and Unexpected Gift).

Don't...

... discount or ignore this lesson because you feel radically different about it.

... assume you know what she wants without first checking it out.

... wait until the last minute to make plans to celebrate the Big Five.

LESSON 4

Understand Your Wife's Perspective about Sex

Thursday, September 27

Walking into my gym before I meet with clients this morning, I immediately can tell someone has been here to clean. There's a sticky note on my small desk in the corner: "My cleaning crew was cleaning some of my nearby offices and had 30 extra minutes so I sent them over to your place. Hope they did a good job! K.W."

My landlord, Kevin White, who gives me this space in exchange for personal training, continues to show generosity to me. From his apparent lifestyle, Kevin seems to be in a different financial strata than all my other clients. He drives a six- or seven-year-old Buick, and his clothes are never pressed or starched the way most of my other clients' clothes are. Recently, he told me about a trip he took and mentioned he stayed in a Holiday Inn, whereas my other clients stay in hotels like the Waldorf Astoria. In addition, he recently described a summer camping trip on which he took his grandson; my other clients take their grandkids to Hawaii, the Bahamas, or the Grand Caymans.

Getting ready for my first client, I think about how successful my current business is. Four new referrals called me last week. My current niche of Dallas multi-millionaire baby boomers (with the possible exception of Kevin White) are more than happy to spend $75 an hour so I can teach them how to turn their guts into six-packs. The monthly $750 to $900 each client pays me is mere pocket change for them in exchange for reclaiming their youthful physique.

Five days a week at 7:30 a.m., 9:00 a.m., 10:30 a.m., 12:30 p.m., 2:30 p.m., and 4:00 p.m., I train a rich dude. That's approximately $450 a day I bring in—which is more like $2,000 a week because of cancelations since my high-rolling clients frequently travel. Not too shabby for a personal trainer. However, when I find an investor to fund my gyms, I'll join the ranks of the rich guys I currently train. Me, Jason York, owner of the most awesome line of life-changing gyms ever. My energy rises with the thought of my future success.

Driving into my garage after a long day, I think about the night ahead of me. Although nothing has changed in how Christina treats me, I remember that the Genie keeps harping on the idea that I'm to focus on *how I love and give* instead of focusing on *how I'm loved and given to.*

After the kids are in bed, Christina takes a bath and gets ready for bed. Since Christina's birthday is in a couple of weeks, the thought that now would be a good time to attempt a conversation about the Big Five crawls forward in my mind. I don't want to, but here goes.

"Christina, your birthday is coming up. I thought maybe you would like to go out to dinner to celebrate. Maybe we can get your mom to take care of the kids."

"I'd like the kids to go with us when we celebrate my birthday," she says. "They're my favorite people in the world."

Oooooookay. She's always complaining about how exhausted the kids make her, but fine, if she wants the kids to go. That ruins any adult alone time, but if that's what she wants, fine.

"If the kids are going, then maybe we can go to Moe's or Chipotle," I suggest. She looks down and doesn't say anything.

"It looks like you want to go to a nicer restaurant since it's your birthday." I'm adding up the cost in my mind of two adults and three kids at a moderately priced restaurant.

She looks up. "Yes, I would."

"Okay, what about Macaroni Grill? The kids can eat pizza."

"I'd like that," she says. "The children need to learn how to start eating with good manners in restaurants."

Since the kids are only five, three, and one, there's plenty of time for etiquette training, but it's her birthday, and if that's what she wants, okay.

"What would you like me to get you for your birthday?" I ask.

"I don't know," she says.

"Would you like a new sweater?" I suggest.

"No, but I need some new boots for fall," she says. "I found these boots that I would love." And four seconds later, she's showing me a picture on her smartphone.

"How much are those?" I ask. This Genie is going to break me.

"Normally, they are $150, but they are on sale at Zappos for $75," she says.

$75? Thirty-five dollars is more in line with what I had planned on spending.

"Great," I lie. "Can you text me that link please?"

"Really?" she asks. "That's so thoughtful, Jason."

Yup, that's me, the thoughtful Casanova.

Christina is smiling. She's actually smiling. Wow, the woman is still pretty when she smiles.

"All right, we've got a plan. Next Wednesday," I say and smile back.

"It's next Tuesday, not Wednesday," she says.

"I knew that; I just got mixed up for a second," I lie again. "Next Tuesday."

At least she liked that birthday conversation. Her expression was happier than I've seen in a long time. And though I'm not very happy about wasting seventy-five dollars on some stupid boots, I have to keep remembering that women like nonsense like that.

This marriage is far from full recovery, but that was another positive sign from Christina. She was pleased with my celebration exploration.

What else was on the Genie's "how-to-celebrate-a-birthday" list? A cake and a card? Didn't he even say mushy card? I don't know if I can stomach getting a mushy card. I guess I'll go to Hallmark tomorrow and see what I can find. I better get some sex out of this; that's all I know.

Christina is exhausted and immediately falls asleep. I'm not tired yet, so I wander into the kitchen to find something to eat. And there, sitting on the counter is the Genie, waiting for me.

"I thought this would be a good time to discuss our next lesson," he says.

Grabbing a jar of nuts from the pantry, we both head to the den and sit down. I offer him some nuts, but he declines. Nuts are high in omega-3s, but maybe genies aren't into nutrition.

"The lesson tonight is *Understand Your Wife's Perspective on Sex*," he begins.

Sex is always a welcome topic, I think, as I remember how needy and deprived I am in this area.

"Of course, if both spouses have a mutual appetite for sex, this is an unnecessary lesson. But study after study repeatedly shows that most men have a much stronger desire for sex than women."[11]

Christina's appetite for sex is closer to disgust than desire. That couldn't be normal.

"Today I will not focus on positions in sex or specific techniques—although that conversation is important—but I will discuss a few principles and thoughts that help men understand sex from the female perspective. When a man understands how most women feel—and then makes appropriate accommodations to his wife—this area can become incredibly satisfying."

Sure. Right. And there's a brand-new Beamer in the driveway that's mine.

---

11. After working with hundreds of marriages, it seems like only 80 percent of marriages are like this traditional gender model. In Julie's groups of women, clearly 20 percent had a higher sex drive than their husbands. Have your wife read chapter 32 in *Wife School* if you are in the 20 percent of men with a lower sex drive than your wife.

"There are four sub-points to our topic, Understand Your Wife's Perspective about Sex. Understanding the feminine mindset on sex will put you in a rare league of husbands."

I bet I already know all of the tomfoolery that he's getting ready to tell me. I'm probably already in the league.

"The first point I'd like to make about a wife's perspective on sex is that women feel like sex is an invasion of their most intimate and private parts *unless* certain conditions are first met," he says.

"Invasion?" I ask. "That's the way the female body was designed." That's not my fault.

"In order for women to desire this invasion," he says, "they have a list of stipulations that they first want met. Many wives think they should only have sex with their husband if he *deserves* it. In other words, *many wives only want to have sex if her husband has been, in her opinion, a good husband.*"

"That's garbage, pure garbage," I protest loudly, hoping I don't wake Christina. "That is the most outlandish, offensive, and ridiculous thing you've said. The one huge expectation I had when I married Christina was for regular and frequent sex. Now you're telling me that she's measuring my performance as a husband to see if I deserve it? And I suppose she sets the standards and then evaluates my conduct? Judge, jury, and executioner. I've heard of this."

My ranting doesn't faze him. "I've told you before—in *Husband School* we are trying to learn how the average woman thinks and feels. I am definitely not saying this is *correct* thinking on wives' part. In fact, when I teach *Wife School* to women,[12] I teach them how *men feel* about sex. But again, in *Husband School*, I am alerting you how most women feel."

"Women *owe* their husbands sex. She is the wife, and she was created for me."

"Yes, she was created for you to assist you in serving the Creator. And yes, sex is a very important part of marriage. But just to be clear, she was

---

12. Ask your wife to read chapter 8 in *Wife School*, so she can understand *your* perspective on sex.

not created to be an on-call concubine."

I have had just about all I can take of this *Husband School* trash.

"Again, I repeat that I'm not saying this thinking of many wives is *correct*," he reiterates. "I am merely stating *reality*. When you understand that your wife has a different perspective about sex, then you can begin to negotiate and discuss this important area."

My perspective is that I'm saddled with a frigid wife whom I wish I could exchange for a hot babe.

"When your wife feels loved, cherished, and known (which she will after you give your garden these eleven secrets), then she will feel like you *deserve* sex."

"No husband can ever give to the extent that you recommend," I plead. "No husband."

"Women do not demand you are a perfect husband," he says, "but they must feel your honest attempt and effort at trying to love, cherish, and know them if you want them to be willing and engaged sex partners. They may give you sex even if they don't feel known and cherished, but their heart will not be in it."

I feel weak hearing this. How does any man give his wife all this repeated baloney? I thought I was making progress in *Husband School,* but now I want to gag again.

"The second thought I want to present tonight is that wives do not want to have sex if they feel threatened in any way by other women," he says. "You, as a man, desire multiple sexual partners, I know. But any evidence of your desire for other women is immensely offensive to your wife."

"I don't see why," I say. "I'm only window shopping." I do look at porn sometimes, but that's not like having an affair. I haven't had an affair...eh...yet. Guilt slams me, though, as I know how unfaithful I am in my sexual appetites.

"When you check out women's bodies with your eyes, your wife is offended. If you light up around an attractive woman, your wife is repulsed. Anytime your wife senses that you are attracted to another woman, she is saddened. She doesn't understand your sexual appetite. In your mind, since you *somewhat* corral your sexual appetite (by not sleeping with other women), you think you're giving her a great gift, the gift of sexual faithfulness. But your desire for other women, even though you don't *outwardly* act on it, is apparent to her and hurts her deeply."

After the Victoria Secret ad came on TV one Sunday afternoon while we were watching the Cowboys, Christina said, "I can see your heart racing in your chest from here" and got up and left the room. Later, I wondered if her extreme coldness for the next few days was somehow related to that. Gosh, I was *only* looking.

"Whenever you show interest in any woman at all, your wife will be wounded. She especially will not want to have sex with you because then she doesn't feel adored and safe."

Another memory flashes to my mind, this one of Chelsea, a friend of mine, showing interest in me at a party a few months back. Later, Christina got all over my case, because she said I "enjoyed it." I mean, who doesn't like an attractive woman being excited by him? Can I help it if I'm a natural born babe magnet?

"So what am I supposed to do if an attractive woman shows attention to me?" I ask, explaining to the Genie my helplessness if this should happen again.

"Immediately, you put your arm around your wife, or hold her hand, or put your hand on her knee," he says. "This behavior acknowledges to the world (and to your wife) that you are not interested in the woman who is showing you attention, and that you are delighted with your wife."

But that's a lie. I'm not delighted at all.

"In a woman's mind, trustworthiness is the most important quality for a husband to possess. It's a three-alarm fire if you demonstrate that you are excited by another woman.[13] Similarly, a wife becomes especially

---

13. This goes both ways. If you've ever seen your wife light up and be excited around other attractive or successful men, you know how painful it is. Both spouses instinctively know their affections belong to one another.

irate if you spend any time alone with an attractive woman."[14]

Christina would die if she knew how attracted I am to Delaney.

"Let's discuss a third principle regarding women and their perspective on sex. Men are stimulated by the sight of a woman's body, as you well know."

I love a woman's body like I love fried chicken: breasts, thighs, and legs.

"Women are *not* sexually stimulated by a man's body parts at all, especially not his penis."

That's my favorite body part. That's the king, the governor, the royalty.

"In fact, not only is she *not* turned on by seeing your nakedness," he says, "but if you don't give her these eleven non-negotiable nutrients, she will see your penis as a one-eyed snake."

"That couldn't be true, Genie. That's the best part of me."

"I know men feel this way, but the truth is, women feel completely different," he says.

Wow. I mean, wow. This has turned out to be a very sad day.

"Your sex organ is six inches below your waist," he says. "But your wife's sex organ is her brain. You have to figure out what she wants. Praise makes some women feel sexy. Other women, to get in the mood, want you to help with the dishes,[15] read books to the children,[16] or have an intimate conversation.[17] There are only a few items on her list, however, to be checked off. It is not an inexhaustible list."

Her inexhaustible list exhausts me.

"When she feels you are trying to love her in a language she can hear, her brain—her sex organ—will choose to respond to you. The codes to unlock

---

14. The human body was designed so that sex hormones are stimulated (almost always) whenever a man is alone with (what he considers to be) an attractive woman. Therefore, it is prudent that men are not alone with an attractive member of the opposite sex for any length of time. Wise husbands do not hire highly attractive assistants, as this would present daily temptation. (You already understand this, don't you?)

15. See Lesson 5.

16. See Lesson 7.

17. See Lesson 1.

her mind are in your words and actions. Foreplay to a woman includes a lifestyle of continuous attention, compliments, and thoughtful acts."

Words and actions arouse women? I thought walking around the bedroom naked would turn Christina on. I wish she would walk around naked.

"Men get stimulated over almost anything," he says. "The almost constant desire for sex reigns in many men's bodies. But in contrast, to a woman, a lifestyle of giving her *attention* is the foreplay she wants. A wife wants you to flirt with her, tease her, notice her, be interested in her, and compliment her. Foreplay to a wife is the *daily attention* you give her to make her feel beautiful, desirable, wanted, and admired."

Instead of seeing Christina as someone to flirt with, I see her as if I'm a trial lawyer, and she's the trial lawyer on the opposing side.

"Let's talk about hygiene for a moment," the Genie says. "Many wives often like to have a little time to take a bath before they have sex. But mainly, wives want *you* to shower, brush your teeth, and perhaps shave. If women smell any type of offensive odor, they do not want sex."

"How ridiculous!" I say, severely annoyed. "Cave men didn't do this. Men have never done this. Men simply want to nibble on her neck, and then they want their woman to immediately roll over and become a ravishing lover."

"You are again correct that this is what *men want*," he says. "But to women, sex is the culmination of a great relationship, of trusting you, of having much conversation, and of feeling loved, cherished, and known. Being nibbled on the neck or having her sexual organs groped without these prerequisites is repulsive to wives."

I'd love to be groped in the right places.

"Another thought is that a wife's sexual desire is often based on how desirable she feels, and guess who largely determines that?" he asks.

He's not pinning her psychological dysfunction on me. "I thought everyone was responsible for their own thoughts and feelings," I say, rebutting his accusation.

"Yes, they are. But marriage is different. The two become one. She is intertwined with you in a way that most humans cannot understand. How *she thinks you view her* has a great impact on how she feels about herself. And if she feels desirable, she wants sex."

So I'm in charge of filling up this insecure woman's ego? Is there no end to my responsibilities? Whatever happened to the old two-way street metaphor?

"The fourth perspective of women we will discuss tonight is that you must be a student in how to sexually stimulate and satisfy your particular wife," he says. "Every wife has a sex manual in her heart, but you must discover it. Men are reluctant to expend this energy because they mistakenly think that men should be natural-born lovers, and should by nature, know how to delight a woman. There could be nothing *further from the truth*. A man is born with no more knowledge about satisfying a woman than he is born knowing how to maintain an automobile. But unlike your car, your wife can talk. Ask her what she likes and doesn't like, and don't be offended when she tells you."

Maybe most men need this, but I'm an awesome lover by nature.

"Ask her if she likes it when you kiss her breasts. Ask her how much foreplay she likes," he says.

One time I saw a guy kissing a girl behind the knees in a movie, so I did that with Christina. How humiliating it was when she told me to stop.

"Men don't come with lovemaking software," he says. "They come with software for eating, sleeping, and ejaculating, but not lovemaking."

"Why doesn't she just tell me what she wants?" I ask.

"Because she is under the misconception, too, that you should know. In addition, she's just trying to get you to watch less TV and help with the kids. She instinctively knows she can't ask for everything, so she doesn't ask for better bedroom skills. You will not know what she wants without exploration, listening, and communication."

Our infrequent sex is not about any failure on my part. It's about her North Pole sexuality.

"Know that all husbands have to learn their particular wife's preferences in order to love her in a satisfying way. There is no one thing that all women want during lovemaking. Every man must extract his wife's individual playbook from her mind. Sometimes women want you to take them. Other times, they want you to round the bases, taking it slow and easy."

No real man does this. *Husband School* is for henpecked wimps.

"Many couples like to schedule sex for the same time each week,"[18] the Genie says. "Having a scheduled time each week in which a couple knows when they will have sex takes a lot of pressure off many wives. Couples can then guard the time and energy needed for sex."

"Scheduled sex? I want sex when I want it!" I nearly shout.

"Yes, I know," he says. "But how is that working for you? You ask Christina for sex all the time, and she turns you down. Scheduling sex *at a good time for her* would ensure a certain amount of sex for you each week. Many couples have found scheduling sex a lifesaver for their marriage."

I should get sex when I want it, not on some stupid schedule. I bring home most of the bacon; she should bring the sizzle in the bedroom on my demand.

"Since she is the one who has to have so many conditions right (and you can be ready on a moment's notice), why not negotiate how many times you will have sex each week and then let her pick the times?" he suggests.

Scheduling sex? How outrageous and ridiculous.

"The next point I'd like to make is tangential to our subject on sex today," he says, "but nevertheless, an important one. After marriage, many men only touch their wife when they are thinking about sex. When sexually stimulated, men are quick to grab their wife's buttocks or fondle her breasts. But randomly grabbing a woman's sexual organs is unpleasant to her."

I thought all women but Christina loved that!

"Women do adore touching, but they want Nonsexual Touching.

---

18. Many couples cannot conceive of scheduling sex. This suggestion is for couples who struggle with different amounts of sexual desire as well as busy couples who need to protect their intimate time together.

They like to hold hands, hug, kiss, pat, and rub, but at times when you're not trying to get sex."

How else does a man let his wife know it's time to produce the goods?

"Your wife wants Nonsexual Touching to be an expression of affection, not just a gesture so you can get sex."

Who wants to touch unless he's going to get some action?

"Nonsexual Touching is incredibly important to wives in order for them to feel cherished by you," he adds.

I feel nauseous again.

"The last topic of the night is not specifically about your wife's perspective on sex, but it definitely affects your marriage. The topic is porn."

Another streak of guilt shoots through me. I know porn is wrong, but it's quick, it's exciting, and it's on demand.

"Men were never created to see naked women's bodies or even half-dressed women's bodies before marriage. They were designed so that the first time they encountered a naked female body, it would be on their wedding night."

Our Sunday School class recently had a swimming party. It was fun checking out all the other women's butts and breasts in their skimpy bikinis.[19]

"Porn enables a man to not only have sex on demand but also to have sex with multiple partners at one time. Porn teaches men that sex includes exotic outfits and experiences so that simple sex with his wife no longer satisfies him. Porn devastates marriages."

I know porn is wrong, but I excuse it because Christina does not take care of my sexual needs. As I think about my sexual fantasies, what I'd really like is not to have any fences or limits around my sexuality at all, so I could satisfy my sexual craziness whenever and however I wanted. I know that's wrong,[20] but I'm just saying…

---

19. The church needs to wake up about modesty!
20. God has created you and given you His set of rules that protect and bless you. Not playing by the rules is a direct insult and rebellion to Him, demonstrating to Him that you will not comply with His commandments. If you are struggling with porn, the answer is to repent immediately and to renew your mind with the Word, learning how the Lord of the universe wants you to behave with your sexuality. There is no excuse for a Christian man to ever look at porn.

The Genie dissolves and departs while I dejectedly walk to the bedroom to go to bed. Checking my phone before I fall asleep, there is a text message from Delaney: "I thought about you at 4 p.m. today and missed our workout. I'm so excited about our meeting on Monday!"

Looking at my sleeping wife, I wish she was as delighted with me as Delaney appears to be.

I text back, "See you then." Guilt floods me, but I tell myself, This is business. I turn off the light as I turn off my conscience.

SUMMARY OF LESSON 4

Understanding Your Wife's Perspective about Sex

Do...

    . . . realize that most men have a higher appetite for sex than women.

    . . . realize that your wife only wants to have sex with you if she feels that, in her opinion, you have been "a good husband." (Although this is incorrect thinking on women's part, this is how they often feel.)

    . . . realize that your wife must feel your honest attempt to love, cherish, and know her if you want her to be a willing and engaged sex partner.

    . . . realize that women are highly offended if you show any interest in other women.

    . . . realize that a woman's sex organ is her brain. A lifestyle of attention, making her feel beautiful, desirable, important, and wanted, is the foreplay she desires.

    . . . consider scheduling if you and your wife desire different amounts of sex, or if you are very busy and need to protect your intimate time together.

    . . . realize that women adore Nonsexual Touching when you aren't trying to get sex.

Don't...

. . . expect your wife to be turned on by your nakedness, of being nibbled on the neck, or by having her sex organs groped.

. . . expect to naturally know how to sexually stimulate and satisfy your wife.

. . . think porn is harmless. In contrast, it's devastating to your marriage and repugnant to the Lord.

LESSON 5

Understand How Your Wife Feels about Managing the Household

Monday, October 1

Christina is frazzled again this morning, as she usually is on days she works. In addition to trying to get herself ready for work, she can't find one of Mason's shoes, Isabella is whining about not liking her "ugly backpack," and Samantha refuses to eat breakfast. Christina repeatedly complains about the chaos of these mornings, saying how hard it is to get two kids to daycare, one to school, and be on time for work herself. I don't complain about the hard things in my life.

Walking into my gym before I get started with my morning clients, I notice there are sacks of cauliflower, broccoli, and cabbage on my desk, along with a sticky note from my landlord: "Jason, here are some good carbs for you from my garden! Thanks for retraining my mind about food! K. W." Fresh vegetables from the garden are hard to beat.

The morning passes quickly, and I head to Modern Market in Preston Hollow to meet Delaney for lunch. She is already there, and immediately I know I've made a mistake by agreeing to meet her. Her low-cut top tells me this is not all business. I wonder if I'm a rabbit getting ready to meet with the fox.

"So what are the goals you wanted to talk about?" I ask, after we get our food and sit down. My eyes are having trouble avoiding the cleavage popping out of her shirt. My body feels as though it is being hijacked.

"I wanted to talk about my body and how you think I could take it to another level," she says, looking at me coyly out of the sides of her eyes.

"I'm not sure how to improve your workouts or your diet, Delaney. You're already a picture of perfection." I didn't mean that the way it sounded. I only meant there is not much more I can do to improve her physique, but it sounded like I am a fawning teenager. Delight is all over her face. What a bonehead thing to say.

She smiles and waits to see if I'm going to say something else. She looks down, sips her water through her straw, and then looks back at me. Though my body is bursting with excitement, my conscience is shouting, "Danger, danger, danger."

"You're probably the best trainer in the whole country, Jason," she gushes.

Obviously, that remark pleases me, so I tell her a little about my prior dream of owning three gyms by the time I was thirty, but that I'm behind schedule now. Then I tell her a little about my meeting with Charles Bateman (I don't give her his name) and how disappointing the 90/10 split was. She listens very attentively, strongly encouraging me. I wish Christina would listen and praise me like this.

My text message goes off, and it's Christina. "Your mother texted me and wants to know what week she can come. Haven't you talked to her about our three-night agreement?"

My mother! I forgot to call my mother and discuss her visit. I text back: "Busy with a client. I'll call her ASAP."

Glancing at my watch, I realize I need to leave because I have another client to train. While excusing myself and standing to leave, I watch as Delaney flips me a provocative smile.

Walking to my car, I know that being alone with Delaney is like a bear walking into a trap. She is putting herself out there for me, like a plump roast chicken on a platter, ready to be carved and consumed. But what can I do? Since I train her father and two of his friends, it would be bad business to quit training her. Driving back to my gym, my Middle Eastern friend shows up in the passenger seat.

"You need a cold shower, Young Jason."

Ignoring the remark, I reply dryly, "She's a client."

Likewise, he ignores my comment and begins. "Today's subject is Understand How Your Wife Feels about the Burden of Managing the Household."

"The burden of the household?" I ask. "She complains all the time about the housework, the cooking, and the laundry, but that's her job!"

"In addition to household management," he adds, "Christina works outside the home twenty hours a week and takes care of three little children."

I can already tell I'm not going to like this lesson.

"Of course, not all women feel a burden with managing their household," he says. "But when women feel they don't have much free time, yet *notice their husband has adequate discretionary time* for hobbies, TV, relaxation, and sports, they become quite upset."

Those are unalienable rights, given to men in the Constitution.

"Men are notorious for letting their wives assume all of the traditional female roles in addition to working outside the home or homeschooling," he says. "If your wife feels overworked, she is going to be unhappy if you do not offer to help relieve her—either by helping her yourself or by hiring help. Otherwise, her irritation will show up in disrespectful speech as well as coolness in the bedroom."

Women should just suck it up and get the housework done.

"You need an honest conversation with Christina about her workload," he suggests. "Couples must negotiate a division of labor in their marriage. I have compiled a list of most of the tasks needed to run a household."

He hands me a piece of gold parchment paper. I silently read the list:

Common Household Tasks

Daily: Working to provide income. Childcare. Cooking. Dishes. Tidying up. Emptying trash. Packing lunches. Driving kids to school. Helping with homework. Taking kids to after-school activities. Pets. (Possibly homeschooling or taking care of elderly relatives).

Weekly: Cleaning (bathrooms, dusting, vacuuming, picking up, mopping floors, changing sheets, etc.) Laundry. Planning menus. Grocery shopping. Errands. Paying bills.

Seasonally: Doctor and dental appointments. Taxes. Car maintenance. Yard and garden care. Planning vacations. Cleaning the refrigerator. Cleaning windows. Cleaning the garage. Home repairs. Computer repairs. Handling insurance. Planning birthdays, Christmas, and holiday events. Entertaining. Making investments.

After reading that list, I know Christina assumes responsibility for the large majority of those tasks. But she's the woman. She's supposed to.

"One secret men have used for centuries to support their wives with their workload," the Genie says, "is that they offer to help their wives with tasks *they don't detest.*"

But I hate them all.

"In my experience with husbands," he says, "many men don't mind grocery shopping, running errands, or taking kids to appointments. Other jobs men don't despise are cooking and laundry. It seems like the task of cleaning is what irks most men. Maybe if you offer to help Christina with some of the tasks on the list *that are not repugnant to you*, she will do the cleaning. But maybe not. Maybe help with the cleaning is what she really wants. Again, this is a conversation you must have."

I don't care if she wants help with cleaning or not. I draw the line there.

"The inescapable and unavoidable truth is that you have a choice: relieve your wife from being overworked or have a resentful wife," he says.

The rope around my neck is tightening, and I find it difficult to breathe.

"The cost for you to ignore this lesson is very high, Young Jason. Women often feel anger toward a husband who doesn't protect her from the household's overwhelming responsibilities. How much smarter if together, you attempt to get her workload to a manageable level."

"Christina would never be satisfied," I say. "Even if I volunteer for a couple of those jobs, she will still interrupt me during a football game and ask me to watch the baby or unload the dishwasher."

"Of course, you can explain to Christina how you feel about relaxing and having uninterrupted time while you watch a game. But negotiating the workload is an important part of marriage to most wives. Men don't want to discuss this subject because they are decidedly opposed to doing what they consider to be traditional female work."

Why combat history?

"I'm just telling you how wives think," he says, "You can argue about whether it's right or wrong if you want. But if Christina feels overworked while you have ample discretionary time—and you don't make an effort to protect her or help her solve her dilemma—she will pull away from you emotionally and sexually."

Unbelievable. If I don't treat her with white gloves, she acts like a spoiled child.

"I counsel men to negotiate a plan that's palatable to both spouses," he says. "Sometimes, this entails hiring household help."

"Who can afford that?" I ask incredulously.

"Couples must decide on their values," he says. "Some couples would rather drive older cars, live in a smaller house, and not go out to eat, in order to afford household help."

My car is eight years old now, and we rarely eat out. No money there.

"In summary, Young Jason, if a wife is overworked while you relax, she interprets this as you not caring about her. Giving your wife all of the eleven nonnegotiable secrets in *Husband School* makes a wife feel cared for, cherished, and loved. For centuries, men have desired a loving, warm, encouraging spouse *without* paying the price of the eleven non-negotiables. These laws are written, however, in a woman's heart and you cannot override them, no matter how rich, handsome, smart, or witty you are."

I'm everything in that list except rich.

The Genie swirls into a funnel of smoke and dissolves. What a miserable lesson. There must be a way around the nonsense this clown suggests.

Almost home, I still have time to call my mom. Maybe she won't answer.

"Hello, Jason," my mother says. "I am so glad it's you, so we can plan my trip. Christina won't text me back."

"Hi, Mom," and we begin an uncomfortable conversation about her only staying three nights, a conversation in which she accuses me of being selfish, rude, and an ungrateful son. Repeatedly, I try to tell her that our house is crazy right now with three little kids and anything longer than a three-night stay throws us into overdrive.

"I've never heard of children telling their parents how long they can stay," she says. She hangs up, and I'm hopeless again. Bossy women drain the life out of me.

Christina and I arrive home about the same time. She's back from picking up car pool, and the two older kids are already out of the car. It seems like they're high. Christina knows better than to give our kids sugar.

While Christina struggles to get backpacks and diaper bags out of the car, I take a call on the driveway about a change in next Saturday's rec league schedule. Walking into the kitchen, I notice it's an absolute mess. I wish she would clean up the dishes as soon as we use them.

While Christina begins to unpack the kids' bags, I explain to her that I talked to my mom and told her she could only stay three nights. Christina softly looks at me. "Thank you, Jason. I really appreciate that." Then she adds, "I've noticed you're trying to be sweet lately. It means a lot to me."

Really? She's noticing? That's the only nice thing Christina has said to me about my role as a husband in months. The Genie's talk about offering to help Christina with the household tasks comes to mind. I don't want to offer to help because she still doesn't deserve it, but I guess I'll give this a try.

"What are you doing the rest of the day?" I ask.

She lists taking Isabella to the dentist, grocery shopping, helping Isabella with her homework, and cooking dinner. I do have an empty slot this afternoon in which a client is out of town. Though I had planned to work on my golf game during that time, I choke out an offer: "I can take Isabella to the dentist. I have a client who's out of town, so I have a little more time than usual." I have clients out of town all the time, but no need for complete transparency right now.

Christina is shocked. "What's going on?" she asks.

"I know you have a lot on your plate, and you need some help." Offering *to do things I don't hate* is a step.

Again, pleasure is all over her face.

In the dentist waiting room, Isabella wants to sit in my lap and have me read to her. She keeps putting her chubby little hands on my arms and repeatedly chuckles at the story. She's an exceptionally cute kid.

After the dental appointment, I quickly take Isabella home because I have a client appointment at 4:30 p.m. While dropping her off, I tell Christina I can start taking Isabella to school on the days she works.

"That would help so much," she says. She walks up and gives me a hug and a kiss on the cheek. I can't remember the last time she did that.

Maybe I'll even consider offering to help with the grocery shopping, but I need to think about it some more before I make that commitment. I bet I could figure out how to use Kroger's online Click List, and it would only take a few minutes.

Before I leave, Christina asks, "Have you been thinking anymore about letting me get pregnant again?"

Gosh, I do a nice thing, and then she hits me up again for another baby.

"Christina, can you let that baby thing go? You know I don't want any more kids," I say, obviously annoyed.

She is disappointed with my answer, but I walk out the door anyway.

My text message sound vibrates. It's Delaney. I wonder what she wants now.

"I talked to my dad about possibly partnering with you in your line of gyms. He wants to meet with you to discuss it. When would be a good time?"

I'm flabbergasted. Astonished. Wow. Thomas Rutherford is interested in my line of gyms? I knew the guy was loaded, but since I find him cold and aloof, I've never thought about approaching him to become a financial backer.

I text back: "That's amazing. I really appreciate this, Delaney. What about next Monday, Oct. 15 at 2 p.m. or 3 p.m.? Would either of those times work for your dad?"

In a few moments, she texts back: "Dad said 3 would work. You and I would get to work together since I'm in charge of my father's new business ventures. How fun would that be!"

As I read that text, I immediately know I'm stepping into quicksand if Delaney and I would be working closely together. Strong, suffocating quicksand.

Ignoring her last remark, I text back: "I will email your father some preliminary data, so he can review it at his convenience. Please thank your dad and tell him I'm very appreciative of this opportunity."

She texts back: "This is probably going to go very well for you, Jason. You have someone on the inside rooting for you."

Reading her text, I again feel a check in my spirit, especially since I am noticing a slight degree of improvement in my marriage (emphasis on the word *slight*). I know Delaney is not good for me or my marriage. She makes it very obvious that she is interested in being more than just trainer and trainee. As much as I want Rutherford to fund my gyms, I'm apprehensive over what I'm getting into.

But I need Rutherford's money!

SUMMARY OF LESSON 5

Understand How Your Wife Feels about Managing the Household

Do...

. . . realize that women become upset when they have little or no discretionary time, but you have plenty.

. . . realize that if your wife feels overwhelmed with the responsibilities of the household, she expects you to help her solve this problem, either by helping her yourself or hiring some help, and so on.

. . . consider offering to help her with household tasks that you don't mind doing.

. . . consider cutting back on other expenses to hire household help for her.

. . . have a conversation with her to see how she feels about the management of the household.

Don't...

. . . decide that household tasks are traditional female work and refuse to help.

LESSON 6

Understand How Money Management Affects Your Wife

Friday night, October 5

Driving home after work, I receive a text from Christina: "I'm wearing my new boots. I love them!"

Christina did enjoy her birthday celebration last Tuesday. The kids made it a pretty wild event but she liked the mushy card, the cake (for which I forgot candles, but luckily the restaurant had some), and of course, the boots. During dinner, I had made an attempt at Admiration by saying to the kids, "Guys, don't you have the prettiest mother ever?"

Mason replied, "Yef, the pret-ti-est. The verrrrry pret-ti-est." She loved that. On the way home, she told me it was the best birthday she had had in years and thanked me for all the effort. I wanted to say, "You're dang right it was a lot of effort and expense, and I get back zilch."

When we got home and got the kids in bed, I made an effort to have Deep Conversation. I asked her, "What is heavy in your life right now?" She started talking like she was a dam that just developed a huge leak. Out poured a forty-five-minute discussion about how exhausted she is with the kids and the house. During the whole conversation, I wanted to tell her that is her job and to man up...or woman up, or something. But I didn't, as difficult as it was. I just Hit the Ping Pong Ball Back, while looking into her eyes. At the end of her tirade, I proposed that we sit down this weekend and look at all the household tasks and see what we could do to lighten her load. Naturally, she loved the idea.

And guess what? Not only was she appreciative and sweet, but I got some sex. That's right, some s-e-x. After sex, I didn't mind so much spending that money, time, and effort (although I still minded some because I believe wives should give a lot of hot sex without all this over-the-top Genie stuff). The Genie says he is teaching me the art of marriage and to expect it to be difficult but rewarding.

My mind jumps to thinking about working with Delaney if Rutherford is my financial backer. Could I work with her? Not that our marriage has turned around very much, but there is a glimmer of light in the distance.

As I pull into my driveway, a discouraging thought descends that tonight is a couple's wedding shower that Christina and I must attend. Actually, we are one of the six couples hosting the party for the engaged duo. I hate these events. Women used to have showers on Saturday mornings, but now they're dragging their husbands to these things. What's up with that?

Christina is a bridesmaid in this wedding. Her dress cost me $130, her shoes $55, and now, this party is probably costing another hundred. This might be the fifth wedding Christina has been in during the last two years. Her friends are important to her, but really? We have to spend this much money on her friends' weddings? Ridiculous, if you ask me.

Christina went early to the party, so she could help set up. As I walk in, Christina introduces me to a sorority sister from college who is also a bridesmaid, Brittany Omar. Brittany then calls her husband to come over, so she can introduce me to him. "This is my husband, Pete Omar," she says. Looking at Pete, I want to fall through the floor.

"Well, if it isn't Little Guy," he says. My heart sinks as I realize Brittany's husband is Tower.

"You guys know each other?" Brittany asks.

"We've played a little ball together," Tower says innocently in front of his wife.

"What do you do for a living?" Christina asks.

"I own Pump It Up gyms here in town," he says with a swagger, the same way he might have said that he walked on the moon.

I know those sleazy gyms. They are dirty, they are slow in refunding your money when you cancel, and the weight machines are broken half the time. They are a pathetic excuse for a fitness center.

"What do you do?" he asks me.

"I'm a personal trainer," I say. I'm certainly not telling him I'm getting ready to open an award-winning line of gyms that will put his trash out of business.

"Oh, a personal trainer? Can you support a family doing that?" he asks. The nerve. What a jerk.

Before I can answer, Christina asks if I will help outside with grilling chicken breasts for the quesadillas. I'm glad to get away from Pete Omar, a.k.a. Tower. A better nickname would be Idiot.

Before she walks off though, Christina turns to Pete and says, "Jason wants to open a line of gyms, too."

I can't believe she just said that. Why would she say that? I don't want this loser knowing my personal business.

"Open a new line of gyms?" the nitwit asks. "Where? What part of town?"

His tone is unfriendly. Obviously, the owner of dilapidated Pump It Up gyms doesn't want any more competition. Ha, sure, as if his pieces-of-junk gyms would even compare to my state-of-the-art operation.

"The market is a little saturated, man," he continues. "It's not a good time to open a gym. When are you thinking about opening one?"

I want to say, "None of your dang business," but Christina jumps in again. "He's just waiting on some financial backing. He's ready to go as soon as he can get some money."

Is there any duct tape around here for this woman's mouth?

Now, Tower the Jerk is laughing. "Oh, waiting on financial backing? Sometimes that can be a long wait, my boy." And he laughs again.

I'd like to tell him Target sells disinfectant, and he should buy some for his gyms. But I decide not to start trouble at this party.

While walking toward the door to help with the grilling, Tower yells after me. "Hey, Little Guy, good luck to you in finding some money."

I haven't met someone as obnoxious as Pete Omar in a long time. And I've got to talk to my wife about not telling my business. Good grief!

While grilling on the deck, I run into an old fraternity buddy, Chad Hollingsworth. Chad and I played golf many Saturday mornings in college, with the high-scoring friend buying lunch for the low-scoring friend afterward.

Chad brags a moment about his new Cobra Fly-Z golf clubs. Not wanting to be outdone, I tell him about my new Callaway Strata Ultimate golf clubs that I had just purchased last week. Exchanging contact info, we agree to try to meet soon to play golf, with the same agreement that the loser buys lunch.

After Chad walks off, Christina quietly moseys up and looks around to see if anyone can hear her. Deciding they cannot, she whispers, "You conveniently forgot to tell me about buying those golf clubs. I've been asking you for a new headboard for our bedroom for months, and you say there is no money. There seems to be money for what you want," and she walks off. How dare she tell me what I can buy and what I can't!

When the party is winding down, I tell Christina I'm tired and have an early-morning training appointment (eight o'clock is early, isn't it?). She looks unhappy, but I leave anyway since we are in separate cars. I had hoped to get some sex when she got home, but I'm sure leaving early quelled that possibility. I can't wait to talk to Christina about my need for Sexual Release, but the Genie says I can't ask for anything until after all the eleven non-negotiable secrets have been implemented.

When I get home, I pay the babysitter and she leaves. The Genie is sitting on my bed when I walk into my bedroom.

"Tonight's topic is Understand How Money Management Affects Your Wife," the Genie begins.

I'm not sure what he's going to say, but I do know I'm the man, and I'm in charge of the money.

"This is not a lesson on investments or 401(k)s," he states. "It is not even a lesson on spending, saving, or giving. It is a lesson to alert you to the marital harmony that results when correct thinking about finances is embraced—as well as the problems that result if you choose otherwise."

We'd have harmony if I could control her use of her VISA.

"The subject of finances is one of the most conflict-producing topics in marriage," he says. "Who makes the decisions about what happens to the money that comes into the household? How exactly is the money going to be apportioned, as far as spending, saving, investing, and giving?"

That's a no-brainer. I decide all that.

"The norm in marriages is that the primary breadwinner makes these decisions," he says. "Today I will first address households in which the main breadwinner is the husband. Then I will discuss households in which the main breadwinner is the wife."

Right. The main breadwinner makes the decisions, and that's me.

"Let's begin with discussing a household in which the main bread-winner is the husband. It is true that men are called to be the head of the wife.[21] The average man thinks that being the head means he can use his position to organize family life for his *convenience and pleasure*. That thinking is a gross misunderstanding of the meaning of headship in marriage. The person who is the head is in charge, but is in charge of taking *responsibility* for those under him, of serving them.[22] This mentality is diametrically opposite to the common thinking of the average man who assumes that being in charge means giving orders that benefit himself.

---

21. "For the husband is the head of the wife as Christ is the head of the church, his body, of which he is the Savior" (Eph. 5:23).

22. "Just as the Son of Man did not come to be served, but to serve, and to give his life as a ransom for many" (Matt. 20:28).

Men who understand true headship consider their wife's desires, needs, and opinions equal with their own.[23]

Equal with his own? No man thinks like this.

"In contrast, when a husband doesn't consider his wife's opinions about spending, saving, investing, and giving, she feels devalued."

Well, too bad.

"An *imbalance of power* results in a marriage where one spouse's opinions matter more than the other's. Whenever there is an imbalance of power, the weaker spouse resents the one in power. A man mistakenly believes he can manage money *as he pleases* and simultaneously expect sincere warmth from his wife."

I want more than just warmth, Buddy-boy.

"The healthiest way to handle money—but which is extremely rare—is for spouses to quarterly, if not monthly, sit down at a computer screen with a software program such as Quicken or Microsoft Money. Together couples should look at income, savings, spending, investing, and giving. The couple should decide as a team, as a partnership, how to apportion the money. Two sets of values and two sets of preferences must be molded into one. A joint strategy must be created. The negotiating and compromising accomplished in these meetings highly promotes harmony and security in both partners. It is a rare marriage that discusses finances as much as is needed."[24]

We don't discuss sex. We don't discuss money. Mainly, we discuss what's wrong with me.

"Sharing money decisions is difficult for a husband when he is the main breadwinner. But *not doing so* has a high price because a wife will detect this imbalance of power and feel tension toward her husband."

He keeps forgetting about *my* tension.

---

23. "In this same way, husbands ought to love their wives as their own bodies. He who loves his wife loves himself" (Eph. 5:28). (In addition, Lesson 9 expounds on the subject of Leadership.)

24. We highly recommend Dave Ramsey's courses and materials.

"Frequently, a husband is more interested in the subject of finances than is his wife. And often a wife is happy to defer the financial decisions to her husband, especially during the child-rearing years when she is merely glad not to have another responsibility on her plate. But this is unwise. The more both spouses know about the finances, the less conflict there will be. When black-and-white numbers are on a computer screen, it is much easier for both spouses to be realistic."

Christina is ridiculous—not realistic—about money.

"I'd like to address a topic that men often fail to consider when couples are making a budget: a woman's love of beauty. Not only does she want to spend money on making her home beautiful, but she wants to spend money on making herself beautiful (i.e., skin care, makeup, clothes, and jewelry). This love for beauty is in her DNA, so it is of no use for you to resist it. Women often want to paint walls or purchase window treatments, whereas men feel these expenditures are frivolous. Understanding that this desire for beauty is built into women should give men an ability to allow for something in their wives that they don't think is necessary."

Pillows? Thirteen different purses? Antiaging skin cream? Is he suggesting I'm not to be upset over these wasteful purchases?

"Men value cars, nice phones, flat screen TVs, and speed boats, but tend not to value cosmetics, jewelry, or shoes."

How can he compare jewelry with the necessity of a large megapixel flat screen?

"Now we will switch to a discussion about a household in which the primary breadwinner is the wife," he says.

My brother, Edward, is a sculptor and his wife, Emily, is the primary breadwinner. I would hate that arrangement.

"Even with the modern thinking of your current society, where both sexes and roles are equal, women still tend to expect men to shoulder and bear the couple's finances," he continues. "If a husband is in school, his wife is, of course, happy to do the heavy lifting. Or, if a husband is trying to start a business and needs financial support during the initial phase, again, wives are willing to carry the financial load."

I'm trying to start a business, *and* I'm carrying the financial load.

"Also, when husbands are trying to make it as artists or writers and show a very strong work ethic in pursuing their dream, wives are often content to support them while they reach for the stars. What is not tolerated by women, however, seems to be when men putter around the house aimlessly. The reverse traditional roles (where the wife is the main or sole breadwinner) seems to sometimes work in couples when the other role (childcare, cooking, housework, errands, holiday preparations, etc.) is at least somewhat embraced by the husband. But often men don't have antennas or desires for that kind of work, and women are still picking up much of the slack. These same husbands still want frequent sex (men are men), but a wife in this situation is often not interested."

Wives should give sex regardless of other problems in the marriage.

"Much of sexuality in a woman's mind is based on respect and admiration," he says. "Needing to 'parent' a spouse is a huge turn-off for women. When a wife loses respect for her husband, the sex life inevitably suffers greatly."

Christina's coldness is due to something else because I do provide financially.

"A woman in this category is initially drawn to her husband because of his sex appeal, charisma, and humor, but these qualities quickly fade when he isn't providing adequately. If children are involved, resentment grows even higher as the needs rise at home."

I'm not telling my brother any of this.

"Before I leave today, I will close with a few more comments about finances that are pertinent to all marriages," he says. "First, it should go without saying that full disclosure of all income, as well as full disclosure of all expenditures, is necessary. Trust and honesty are the concrete foundation of any relationship. Without honesty, relationships are doomed."

My recent purchase of golf clubs stings me.

"Next, no spouse should ever make a large purchase without the wholehearted consent of the other. The main breadwinner, though, often does not feel a need to consult the spouse about his or her expenditures, but the result is always the other spouse feeling disrespected and offended. A spouse who feels disrespected and offended is low in goodwill toward the other spouse."[25]

This financial lesson is one that this Genie guy is not going to bully me into accepting.

"Finally, it is important to know that couples who *save* together seem to have an easier time in marriage than couples in debt," he says. "Debt is poison to marriage, and everything must be done to tackle it."

"Christina still owes eleven grand for her dental hygienist school tuition," I say. "I mean, she brought that debt into the marriage. Why should I have to pay it off? Her parents should pay it."

"You are now one, Young Jason. Although of course it is preferable if spouses don't bring debt into the marriage, the fact is *they do*, and now as a couple, you must own it together and find a strategy to get rid of it."

Yeah, the burden always comes back to me, myself, and I.

"In summary," he says, "the husband is called to love his wife equally as much as he loves himself. This means her concerns and desires are equal with his. One way a husband demonstrates his love—or his lack thereof—is by how he views and manages money in his marriage." And with that, the Genie is gone.

How tonight's lecture annoyed me. These lessons keep getting worse.

While the Genie was here, my mother called and left a voice mail. Opening it, I hear, "It's very expensive for me to fly to Dallas and only stay for three nights," she begins. I close the voice mail without listening to the rest of it. I'm tired and in no mood to be further criticized.

My text message sound beeps. It's Delaney. "Keep thinking about me helping you build your empire! So thrilling."

---

25. It's very helpful, if possible, if both spouses can have their own discretionary money built into the budget. We call it "Mad Money."

Reading the phrase *your empire* makes me smile. Delaney sure gets me.

When Christina comes home, she tells me she is upset that the other husbands stayed and helped clean up, but I left.

"You're upset with *me*?" I ask in disbelief. "What about *you* telling random people about my future private business plans?" Even though I remember the Genie saying to not criticize or correct Christina until I implement the eleven secrets, I don't care. She crossed a line.

"I was just trying to get a conversation going, Jason. You stand around like you're a statue, not engaging people. Britney is one of my good friends from college, and I was embarrassed by the way you stood there tonight and didn't try to make conversation."

Really? She blabs about my personal stuff, but then *I* get criticized for not being voted Mr. Personality at the party? I thought this stupid *Husband School* might be starting to help a little, but now, I'm ready to ditch the whole thing. Christina is just as contentious as ever. No matter what I do, she criticizes me.

The thought of getting sex tonight was certainly a joke.

The only thing I feel good about is building my dynasty of gyms— but that comes with a temptress.

SUMMARY OF LESSON 6

Understand How Money Management Affects Your Wife

Do...

    . . . realize that the primary breadwinner, when it is the husband, has a tendency to think his opinions about spending, saving, investing, and giving are more important than his wife's.

    . . . realize that when an *imbalance of power* occurs (i.e., when one spouse's opinions matter more than the other's), the weaker spouse resents the one with power.

    . . . realize that using a software program like Quicken or Microsoft Money, and looking at black-and-white numbers on a computer screen together, helps a couple devise a joint money strategy.

    . . . realize that the more both spouses know about the subject of their finances, the less conflict there will be.

    . . . realize that most women always have expected—and most women always will expect—men to shoulder and bear the couple's finances.

    . . . get rid of debt and then purpose to save.

Don't...

    . . . discount a woman's love of beauty just because it's not important to you.

    . . . let your wife lose respect for you by not adequately providing.

    . . . make large purchases without the wholehearted consent of the other.

LESSON 7

Understand How Your Wife Feels about Your Role as a Father

Saturday, October 13

Driving to my rec game, I again realize how much I love basketball on Saturday mornings. It's time to show those young twenty-year-olds who the real man on the court is. I relish the fact that I can still destroy those guys with my killer three-point shot.

My excitement dwindles, however, as I think about the conversation I had last night with Christina about getting on a budget. I purchased Microsoft Money software and asked her if we could sit down together and make a budget. She snidely replied, "A budget? Are you going to let me know when you buy more golf clubs?"

Ignoring her disrespect, I told her we needed to tackle her dental hygienist school debt. Her response was that she still wanted a new headboard for the bedroom and hoped we would soon buy her a GMC Yukon Denali. Those babies cost around sixty grand new. I spend a measly $900 on golf clubs, and she thinks she deserves a $60K car?

Walking into the gym, I am startled to see Tower. Why is he here? He plays on another team.

Upon seeing me, Tower begins to laugh. "Hey, Little Guy is here again. How 'bout that?"

"Hello, Pete," I say and shoot a three. Swish. In your face, Punk.

"I thought you were on another team," I say, still trying to figure out why he's here.

"It's rec league, Little Guy, so I'm subbing to help out a friend. Hey, let's make a bet. Last time we played you were real lucky with your shooting. My prediction is that you score seven points or less today. Wanna put fifty dollars on that?"

Lucky? Trying to keep cool, I garnish every ounce of self-control because what I really want to do is punch him in the face. Since I scored twenty-four points last week, this is a safe bet. He has no idea who he's dealing with.

A couple of my teammates encourage me to take the bet, quietly whispering they will get me the ball. "You're on," I say. No way he can keep me to seven points. My three-pointer is unstoppable.

The game begins. I'm trying to get free to score, but Tower plays dirty and, at one point, grabs my shirt. "Aren't you going to call that?" I ask the ref.

"Call what?" he replies. "One more comment out of you, and you're outta here."

"He's my brother-in-law," Tower whispers as he winks at me.

Tower pushes, elbows, and plays as rough as I've ever seen in rec ball. I can't remember being this angry playing basketball before.

Tower swats down a couple of my shots while he trash talks. I miss most of my usual three-pointers, as not only does Tower guard me closely, but he's in my head.

With sixty seconds left in the game, I've scored only six points. I need two more points to win the bet. My teammates are with me, passing me the ball every chance they get.

"Little Guy, the clock is ticking," Tower taunts. "And man, I'm hungry. I'm going right out to spend your fifty bucks on some tasty lunch." He and his idiot teammates roar with laughter.

With thirty seconds left, I miss a lay-up. Tower and his gang can't stop howling.

Ten seconds, I miss a three-point shot.

Two seconds, I put it up, it's going in, it's going in…but it rolls around the rim and falls off.

I can't believe this moron is going to take my fifty dollars. I can't believe it. I mean, last week, I had twenty-four dang points.

"Little Guy, you just made my morning," Tower says, and all his buddies give him a high five. "Six *little* points for one *Little* Guy." And they howl again.

Leaving the gym, I feel angry and embarrassed, feeling stupid to have lost to such a loser. The disappointment feels like I had just lost the state tournament for my team. I'm certainly not telling Christina I lost fifty dollars in a bet.

Usually I don't work on Saturdays, but one client asked me for a make-up session at 1:00 p.m. today and another asked for a make-up session at 5:00 p.m. Christina especially didn't like that second appointment because Isabella has a dance program tonight. But Isabella's program doesn't begin until six-thirty, so I can easily make that.

After training my 1:00 p.m. client, I drive home, still annoyed at losing fifty dollars earlier today. While stewing, the Genie suddenly appears in my passenger seat. I'm again not in the mood to hear a lesson, but what can I do?

"The topic today is Understand How Your Wife Feels about Your Role as a Father," he begins.

My role as a father? She gets no input on that subject.

"Although volumes can be said about competent fatherhood, today we are going to discuss how a man's involvement with his children affects his wife's feelings toward him," he begins. "Many women rate a man's fathering as one of the most important gifts he gives her. Since women care fiercely about their children, great value is attached to how her husband promotes the welfare of the children."

I can't do everything.

"I'm going to give you a brief overview of what competent fatherhood looks like from a wife's perspective. Because men primarily think about work, money, and sex, they don't often see how their fatherhood skills affect their wife."

Maybe when the kids get older and can have adult conversations, I'll be more interested in them.

"In order to grasp this lesson, you need to understand what happens to a woman when she has her first baby," he says. "Nothing in the world changes a woman so drastically as having a baby. Women say their identity, their priorities, and even their worldview changes after they give birth. A raging fire is but a kitten's breath in comparison with the power of a mother's love for her children."

A little of that love funneled in my direction would be nice.

"A woman does not separate a child's well-being from her own," he says. "In fact, most mothers put their child's well-being ahead of their own. If a man doesn't grasp this force that is comparable to gravity, he cannot understand his wife's heart."

There are some forces equal to gravity operating in my body, too.

"A man who does not understand motherhood can sometimes even be jealous of his wife's attention to her children," he continues. "The wise husband, however, embraces his wife's passionate love for her children, assisting her in providing everything the children need to function well. If you do not show up for the children or you do not strive to give them everything they need, she will be severely disappointed in you."

Disappointed? If I don't do everything right, she is disappointed with me? Who can meet this absurd standard?

"What research now shows is that *the bond between a father and his child* highly impacts his child's social behavior, his or her psychological well-being, and even the development of his or her brain. Wives instinctively know this and, therefore, want each of the children to be closely attached to a strong and nurturing male role model."

I'm sure Christina does want this. She wants to squeeze the tar out of me in every area.

"Since children often feel loved by their father according to *the amount of time* their father spends with them, there is no substitute for a father *spending enormous amounts of time with his children*," he says.

Sure. No problem. I'll just sleep between 1:00 a.m. and 4:00 a.m.

"Actively playing together is an important way to spend time together. Games and sports are all healthy activities. In addition, spending time doing productive activities, like raking leaves or washing the car, builds a bond between father and child. A third way to profitably spend time with children is to help them grow intellectually. This can be accomplished by reading aloud to children, helping them with their schoolwork, or being involved with their activities at school. A man often wants to escape the tension of dealing with children, leaving it to his wife, but his children suffer from a lack of close involvement with him. Neither wives nor children adore part-time fathers."

"Christina constantly hovers over the children," I say. "Doesn't she give them enough attention for the both of us?"

"Spending large amounts of time with children is necessary so that the father's values can be caught, values such as hard work, honesty, and service to others. There is no substitute for a father's structured and unstructured time with his children."

Circus Man wants me to have more conversation, celebrate holidays, help with household tasks, and now, babysit. Someone needs to warn my single friends.

"Most men do not have trouble modeling courage, risk-taking, and industry to their offspring," he says. "Where fathers usually stumble, however, is in their lack of demonstrating affection and kindness to their children. Fathers often think it is the mother's role to show these qualities, but children benefit from (and wives adore) a father's affection."

Wimpy, that's what it is.

"Touch the children. Hold the children. Kiss the children. Few men have seen affection properly modeled from their own father. Expressing affection and warmth[26] pulls the hearts of children to their father, as well as the heart of the observant mother. Wives and children have a built-in proclivity to desire time and attention from the father."

There's that vice again, squeezing my head.

"Of course, fathers get frustrated by a child's immature behavior, but this is where men must learn the art of self-control.[27] A father's reaction to his child's disobedience or misconduct is as important as anything else the father does with his child. It is critical that the father learn to control his *voice* and *his hands*. Children need discipline, but it must be done with self-control and patience, two qualities that are difficult for immature men. A father's anger can crush a child. Indeed, fathers model to children how to handle unpleasant situations by how they handle themselves."

Suddenly I remember yelling at Mason and swatting his behind when I was trying to watch a Cowboys game.[28] I almost missed Dak Prescott's game-winning touchdown pass because of that pesky kid.

"You will make mistakes with your children, Young Jason, and it is important you learn how to apologize and ask for forgiveness. This will keep your children's hearts from turning away from you."

I don't apologize to Christina, so it's a stretch thinking I'm going to apologize to the children.

"This is not to serve as a complete dissertation on the enormous topic of fatherhood," he says. "But a wife cares an exorbitant amount about your role as a father. Find a father who seems to have a natural knack for doing this well, and spend time watching how he loves his children. If you can learn to love your children, your wife will be incredibly grateful to you, and her gratefulness will translate to affection and fondness toward you."

---

26. Remember to include the phenomenal relationship-building skills of Colossians 3 in your role as a father: compassion, kindness, humility, gentleness, and patience.
27. "Like a city whose walls are broken through is a person who lacks self-control" (Prov. 25:28).
28. "Fathers, do not exasperate your children" (Eph. 6:4).

I guess I'll be honest here. "Mason is a disappointment, Genie. He doesn't ever want to throw a baseball but only wants to color and cook with Christina. And besides that, he cries easily."

"Just like you don't give love to Christina because she deserves it, you don't give love to your children because they deserve it. Some children, no doubt, can be difficult to love for various reasons. But children who are difficult to love are the ones who need it the most, and you choose to love them because *it is your duty.* The difficult ones are the ones who need extra time, sensitivity, affection, and warmth. You must continually guard against your natural inclinations to *give what is easy* instead of your responsibility to *give your children what they truly need.* It is true that your work and your hobbies provide more immediate satisfaction than spending time with your children. But time with children, especially during childhood, the teens, and even into the twenties, can radically change the direction of a child's life. Nothing is more important in your wife's mind than rearing her children. Therefore, you must continually move toward them, drawing their hearts to you."

Who can do all this? Who?

"If fathers used the same amount of energy to pull their children's hearts to them as they use for their work and hobbies, children would have the lifelong advantage of being close to their father. This relationship results in the child wanting to adopt the father's values and enables the father to continue to influence the child into adulthood." With that the Genie disappears, leaving only a trail of smoke.

Arriving home and walking into the kitchen, I realize I will have to process this lesson later because the household is in chaos. Christina is calling out spelling words to Isabella as she tries to cook something on the stove. She is also feeding Samantha in the high chair while she simultaneously attempts to corral Mason, who is jumping off the coffee table in the hearth room.

What I want to do is walk into the bedroom, shut the door, and turn on the golf channel. Instead, after I change clothes, I return to the zoo and try to help control the wild animals. First, I finish quizzing Isabella on her spelling list, while at the same time, I finish feeding Samantha. I tell Mason not to jump off the table again, and surprisingly, he obeys. The kids then play in the den, so I ask Christina what she plans on doing the rest of the afternoon.

But instead of answering my simple question, she launches into a full-fledged meltdown. First, she tells me about an argument with her mother. Then she rants about Isabella not getting invited to the popular girls' sleepover. And if that's not enough, she describes a phone call this morning that roped her into being in charge of the Christmas program at Isabella's school. Mindful of the principle of Deep Conversation, I repeatedly Hit the Ping Pong Ball Back and we talk for a full thirty minutes. But afterward, I can sense much of Christina's angst and emotional turmoil is reduced. I pull her to me and just hold her, telling her I'm sorry she has so much on her plate. Not being accustomed to this, I can tell she's uncomfortable, and she soon pulls away. Well, so much for that gesture of Nonsexual Touching.

Girding my resolve, I ask what I can do to help. That seems to be the magic question, as Christina's energy instantly rises. She wants me to help with the kids. So I take all three outside to the back yard. Samantha sits in her walker while Isabella, Mason, and I play chase. All three kids are laughing and enjoying our game. Glancing at the window, I see a smiling Christina watching from inside.

After the game, Christina asks me if I would give the kids baths, so I bathe all three, getting them ready for the dance program that begins in a couple hours. I'm hoping for a reward of sex later tonight for my fantastic displays of fatherhood.

In my opinion, though, this whole *Husband School* still sucks. I mean, look at all the giving I'm doing and what has it gotten me? Why, Christina should be nominating me for *Husband of the Year*, and instead, I'm still not getting the sex or respect I want.

The Genie's words appear in my mind: *This is the woman you were given to love*. Well, I won't tell the Genie that the *real* reason I'm motivated to do this is because he also said that after I consistently deposit all eleven non-negotiable secrets, Christina will be open to *what I want*. That's what I'm waiting on, honestly, for some of my needs to be met.

Out of the blue, Delaney and her curves come to mind. What a double-minded man I am. On the one hand, I want to be a good husband, and then, in the next moment, I want Delaney.

After training my 5:00 p.m. client, I change clothes in the gym, so I can head directly to the dance program. In the parking lot, I run into Kyle Stepping, a witty high school buddy who also plays on my rec basketball team. He begins telling me the hilarious story of how his boss repeatedly complains about the hours of lost productivity at work due to the employees spending time on their Fantasy Football teams. We're both laughing at the covert strategies of his coworkers to hide their Fantasy Football involvement.

Kyle's comedy routine made me temporarily lose track of time. Getting into the car, I realize I'm now going to be ten minutes late to the dance program. Surely, ten minutes won't matter.

Walking into the auditorium, I check my phone. There is a text from Christina. "Where are you? Isabella is on!"

That text was sent five minutes ago, so immediately I know I've missed Isabella's dance. I text back: "I'm in the lobby. I got held up. Sorry I missed it. I'll see you at home."

When Christina gets home, she is extremely upset, but she hides her anger since the kids are present.

"Daddy! Where were you tonight? Isabella asks. "Did you see me dance?" Christina tosses me a look like I'm the worst father on the face of the earth. Unsuccessfully, I try to smooth over my ineptitude with an excuse (read "lie") about my work. Christina is unforgiving and remains cool and aloof the rest of the night.

Just before Christina gets in bed, she takes a call from a friend at church as they are both helping with a Christmas party for inner-city kids. Although Christina is a virtuous woman in many ways, she is still a disappointment as a wife. I can't be perfect all the time, but she seems to expect me to be.

There are certainly miles and miles to go in this marriage.

SUMMARY OF LESSON 7

Understand How Your Wife Feels about Your Role as a Father

Do...

>   . . . realize that a man's fathering is one of the most important gifts he gives his wife.

>   . . . realize that the bond between you and your children affects their social, psychological, and even physical development.

>   . . . realize that children feel loved by their father according to the amount of time their father spends with them.

>   . . . express warmth and affection to your children: touch, hold, and kiss them.

>   . . . learn to apologize and ask forgiveness.

>   . . . find a father who loves his children well, and spend time watching how he does it.

>   . . . realize that the time a father spends with his children radically changes the direction of their lives.

Don't...

>   . . . be jealous of your wife's attention to the children. In contrast, assist her in providing everything the children need to function well.

>   . . . react inappropriately to a child's disobedience or misconduct. Instead, use self-control with your voice and especially, your hands. A father's anger crushes a child's spirit.

>   . . . neglect children who are difficult. They are the ones who need your attention the most.

LESSON 8

Understand Your Wife's Desire
for Affection and Romance

Saturday, October 27

Motivated by the Genie's dissertation on fatherhood—as well as my apparent failure to make it to Isabella's recital—I suggested to Christina a couple weeks ago that I sign up Isabella for soccer and volunteer to coach her team. Maybe she'll quit bugging me for another kid if I up my fatherhood involvement.

Christina wasn't so keen on the idea at first, thinking maybe Isabella wasn't the soccer type. "She loves ballet, dolls, and getting dressed up," Christina said.

"She's going to love soccer," I replied with 100 percent confidence.

Since Christina liked the fact that I would be spending time with Isabella, she agreed to my soccer idea. To be honest, I had visions of winning a big trophy at the city-wide soccer tournament for six-year-old girls.

After our first practice last Saturday, though, I knew there would be no trophy. Isabella wanted to hold hands with the other girls and skip around the field. I kept telling her to focus, run hard, and kick the ball, but she said kicking hurt her toes, and she didn't like getting sweaty. With our first game at noon today, my expectations are at rock bottom.

But…drumroll…today is my meeting with Rutherford. Originally, we were to meet on Monday, at 3:00 p.m., but Rutherford changed the appointment to today at four. Four o'clock on a Saturday afternoon seems to me to be an odd time to meet, but Delaney says her father works eight days a week.

I do have one hurdle, however, to get over this morning before Isabella's soccer game and my Rutherford meeting: Christina and I are having our first budget meeting. My hopes for this meeting are even lower than they are for Isabella's soccer game.

In the last couple weeks, I have spent hours recording and categorizing our expenditures over the last six months in the new Microsoft Money software. There are categories for food, household expenses, cars, insurance, taxes, mortgage, medical and dental, entertainment, repairs, clothes, and so on. I also made a list of our earnings for the same period. No matter what I say, I'm sure Christina will—as always—find a way to criticize my efforts.

With two cups of coffee in her hands, Christina walks to the kitchen table. We sit down and stare at the computer screen, which is filled with categories of organized numbers. After looking at the spread sheets together for a few minutes, we are both silent because it is obvious that we are spending all we make, have no savings, and are not reducing her student debt.

"Maybe we should consider selling the house and moving to a smaller one with a smaller mortgage," I suggest.

"Surely there is something else we could do that is not so drastic," she responds, with obvious disdain for my idea. I knew she would be negative about whatever I said.

Silently, she continues to pour over the numbers on the computer screen. "Look how much I've spent on weddings in the last six months. I've spent around four hundred dollars each on four different weddings. This is upsetting, Jason. I had no idea how much we spend."

I refrain, but the urge is strong to say, "How much *you* spend."

"I certainly see there's no money for a new Yukon," she admits. "What are we going to do?" She sadly shakes her head and continues, "I spent forty-five dollars yesterday on some Christmas dishes. I still have the receipt, so I can return them." Pausing, she adds, "I'm sure I can cut out a lot of purchases, if I try."

Christina's reasonableness softens my attitude toward her. I had expected her to be militantly resistant to the entire budget concept.

"Christina, I'm sorry I bought those golf clubs without discussing it with you," I choke out.

With genuine sincerity she responds, "I appreciate you saying that. I think together we can make a big dent in our spending."

Detecting her earnestness in getting on board with the new financial plan, I am somewhat encouraged, and we agree to meet weekly to further strategize. Christina's level-headed reaction to the black-and-white numbers on the computer screen was what the Genie had predicted.

Thoughts from the Genie's talk about being honest with money return to me. So before we adjourn, I make one more confession: "I made a bet during a rec basketball game and lost fifty dollars. That was a bonehead thing to do; I know." I'm ready to receive my tongue-lashing.

"I bet you hated that," she says and laughs. Not only did she not criticize me, but she was sweetly forgiving. What's with that?

Remembering the SUG I ordered, I retrieve it from my trunk and bring it inside.

"What's this?" Christina asks.

"I got you a little something," I say.

"But why?" she asks.

I can't tell the truth, that I'm depositing these eleven nutrients as one would do push-ups. So I say, "A man can't give his wife a gift just because he loves her?"

She is stunned—that's for sure.

Opening the gift, she whispers, "A Michael Kors wallet? Oh my, Jason, I love it!" She unzips all the zippers and runs her fingers over the beautiful white leather. "It's gorgeous, Jason," she softly says, still in shock.

Even I can tell she clearly adores this. I hit the jackpot with the Genie's SUG suggestion.

"I noticed your wallet is falling apart," I say, "and since you have several Michael Kors purses, I thought it was a safe bet." Her look told me everything. She walked over and hugged me.

"Thank you so much. I'm still not quite sure what inspired you, but I really love it." After this, Christina leaves to go to a baby shower.

When the babysitter arrives, Isabella and I depart to our first soccer game. On the way, I attempt to give her a pregame pep talk. I rant about getting back on defense, on running hard, and on staying alert. Isabella is only half-listening, as she has brought her favorite doll, Mary Beth, and is combing the doll's hair. At the end of my remarks, she replies, "Daddy, do you think Mary Beth has pretty hair?"

After we get to the field, I attempt to lead the girls in a warm-up activity, but I might as well have been speaking Chinese. The few that were listening to me didn't understand. Glancing over at the opposing team, a double dose of dread descends on me, just as if you poured a bucket of cold water on my head. It looks like Tower is the coach of the other team! As I watch his team warm-up, there is one tall, slender six-year-old who is obviously Tower's daughter. By the way she can handle the ball, she appears to be on a course to play professional soccer.

Tower sees me across the field and starts laughing. "Well, hello there, Little Guy. We meet again. Which one is your daughter?" I turn and point to Isabella, who, at that moment, is spinning like a ballerina.

"Cute kid. Looks like she's got your focus," he says and walks away.

I want to reply, "Don't let that cute little girl of yours visit your gyms, or you'll be without your best player due to a staph infection." But instead, I regain my composure and attempt to get my straggling team ready to play.

The game begins and Tower's team of Olympic athletes are probably the best six-year-old soccer players in Texas. After scoring three goals, Tower's daughter—whom I'm sure will soon be scouted by major colleges—is again dribbling down the field toward the goal. Isabella is running in the right direction, at least, but trips over her own feet and falls down. Tower starts laughing but again I let it go, even though my blood pressure is probably close to cardiac arrest.

Down near the goal, there is a pile-up of girls, all kicking and going hard after the ball. All of a sudden, I hear a scream and Tower's daughter is on the ground, grabbing her leg. Running over, I say to Tower, "My next-door neighbor is an orthopedic surgeon, and I saw him earlier on the next field with his daughter. I'll get him over here."

In two minutes, Brent Soltic is there, down on his knees, examining Tower's daughter.

"I think it's broken," Brent says. "Would you like me to ask my associate that is on call to meet you at the ER?" he asks Tower.

"Uhhhh, yes, uhhh, thank you," Tower stutters.

"I'll take your other daughter home with me until you are free to come get her," I say to Tower, as I realize his four-year-old is here, too. Britney, Tower's wife, is absent as she is at the same baby shower that Christina was attending this morning.

"Thanks, man," Tower says to me. "I really appreciate it." For the first time ever, his tone is kind and sincere as he is genuinely grateful for Brent's help, as well as mine.

Heading home with Tower's other daughter, Christina texts me that Tower's wife, Britney, has arranged for her mother to meet us at our house and retrieve the younger daughter. Good, because I'm not the babysitting type.

"Daddy, can we have a tea party?" Isabella asks me. Her puffy little cheeks and innocent eyes make my heart explode with affection.

"Sure, honey, but only if your doll, Mary Beth, can come. Is she free this afternoon?"

Squealing with delight, Isabella bursts into laughter as she throws her little arms around me. "Daddy! Of course, she's free! She's a doll!" And she bursts into laughter again.

After the tea party, Christina returns home, and I get ready for my 4:00 p.m. appointment with Rutherford. As excited as I am, there is a cloud hanging over me, knowing how upset Christina would be if she knew how closely I'll be working with Delaney in my new business venture.

I quickly throw on some khakis and a starched French blue shirt for my meeting with Rutherford. I decide a tie is too much for a Saturday afternoon meeting. Grabbing my briefcase, I head out the door for this once-in-a-lifetime event. On the drive to the meeting, I begin to mentally rehearse my presentation, but my thoughts are interrupted when the Genie appears in my passenger seat.

"Genie, I need to prepare for meeting with Rutherford," I say, hoping I can be excused from today's lesson.

"No worries," he says. "Today's lesson is short, although absolutely essential to your marriage. The topic is, Understand Your Wife's Desire for Affection and Romance."

Well, this would be his first short lesson, as opposed to his usually long-winded sermons.

"Have you noticed how women adore love stories? If a man is watching a movie, a love interest makes the movie more exciting because there is an undertone to him of anticipated *sex*. To a woman, there is an anticipated feeling of *romance*."

"Romance?" I ask, somewhat repulsed again. "We have kids, a job, and a mortgage. Let's have sex, watch the World Series, and go to sleep."

"I know that's how *you* feel, Young Jason. But in *Husband School*, I am teaching you how a *woman* thinks, and it is radically different from a man."

I hate being bothered by a woman's wimpy desires.

"This is one of the secrets, Young Jason, that is relatively easy for you to give after you understand it, and it *results in overwhelming benefits to you*. It is beyond me that men have not figured out that if they regularly give their wife Affection and Romance, it absolutely delights her."

"Uh, Genie, didn't we discuss giving Christina words in the Admiration and Appreciation lesson?" Maybe I have a senile Genie.

Laughing, he explains, "Admiration is words that express what a wife does well, and Appreciation is words regarding the benefits she brings to your life. Affection and Romance are words that express your positive feelings for her."

Definitely, overkill.

"After a small amount of time, Young Jason, most couples become like roommates or business associates, with the only difference being some occasional sex. This arrangement is extremely disappointing to wives."

Well, *occasional sex* is extremely disappointing to me.

The Genie continues, "A man once said to me, 'I treat my wife great. I bring home my paycheck, and I even put gas in her car. Besides, I'm not the romantic type. I do things for her to express love instead of using words.'"

Sounds like a smart guy to me.

"Women don't spend billions of dollars on movies to watch (and novels to read) to learn about a man putting gas in a woman's car," the Genie says. "Although this act of service is appreciated by women, it is for scenes of men romancing and wooing women that they spend enormous amounts of money."

Christina does like those sappy romantic movies.

"This desire of women to receive Affection and Romance is true of a nineteen-year-old wife as well as a ninety-year-old wife. A woman never outgrows the desire to feel cherished with Affection and Romance."

After thirty, this nonsense should be over.

"Men usually give Affection and Romance when they have a *sexual urge*, but they are naïve to not realize wives quickly make this association, and realize you are trying to get something. Therefore, you must give Affection and Romance at times when she is persuaded that you are not trying to get sex."

Gonna be a long shot, because I never think about Affection and Romance except when I'm horny.

"We will divide our topic of your wife's desire for Affection and Romance into two categories: words and actions," he says. "We will begin with words. Wives never get tired of *hearing your delight with them personally,* expressed in words. Tell her how soft her skin is, how her eyes still shine. Tell her she still delights you like no one else."

That is what is known as a lie.

"She still wants to feel desirable, cherished, beautiful, adored, and loved by you, and it is impossible to feel this way without a steady stream of *tender words.* You are focused on your career, money, sex, and perhaps a hobby. In contrast, your wife still wants *daily* declarations of your feelings for her."

I'm pretty certain I'm not up for this.

"An example of giving Christina Affection and Romance would be to say at dinnertime, 'Kids, look at your beautiful and sweet mother who cooked us this wonderful meal!' Or you might say to her, 'At the party tonight, you lit up the room with your energy.' Or possibly, in front of your wife, say to your daughter, 'Samantha, you have pretty hair like Mommy.' Other examples might be, 'You look cute in your light green nightgown' or 'Those flowers are bright and cheerful; they remind me of you.' And just remember, you cannot say 'I love you' too often. She wants to hear those words every day."

Too bad. I don't even remember the last time I felt "love" for Christina, so I'm certainly not going to say any of that mushy crapola.

"One husband, away on a business trip in Denver, had the opportunity after his conference, to spend a few hours visiting the Rocky Mountain National Park before his air flight home. He called his wife before boarding the return flight home and said, 'The mountains were beautiful, but I couldn't fully enjoy them, because half of me wasn't here.' This example of Affection and Romance deeply touched his wife."

Actually, I felt that way about Christina when we were first married. But now, I'm almost glad when she's not around.

"Let me remind you that you can also give Christina Affection and Romance with actions as well as words. The two main areas are Good

Manners and Nonsexual Touching."[29]

I can already tell this is going to be a stretch.

"Don't be led astray by the small percentage of women who claim to no longer want displays of Good Manners, as they are still strongly desired by the overwhelming majority of women. Women appreciate having their car door opened for them. When you are out with your wife, she likes you to drop her off at the door, so her hair doesn't get blown by the wind. She likes it when you sense she is cold, and you take off your jacket and wrap it around her shoulders. She loves when you pull out her chair in a restaurant. A woman is delighted when her husband concerns himself with her comfort."

I've got a few ideas about how she could comfort me.

"When she drives up with a load of groceries, it is imperative that you stop what you're doing and help her unload."

"Sometimes I'm in the middle of an important football game on TV," I wail. "I can't stop and help her. Besides, grocery shopping is her job."

"Again, I'm giving you secrets that make huge deposits into Christina's tank, secrets that wildly increase her affection and devotion to you. I didn't say they are always convenient."

I'm not missing Cam Newton throwing a touchdown pass.

"Women also love Nonsexual Touching," he says. Hold her hand as you walk. Reach over, and pat her knee in the movie. Put your arm around her in church. Kiss her cheek, her hands, or the top of her head."

When she gets hot and steamy in bed, maybe I'll consider this.

"I'm getting ready to tell you something that will surprise you, Young Jason. If you refuse to give your wife Affection and Romance, she will be attracted to other men, desiring displays of attention and tenderness from them. She is built with a lifelong desire to be romanced, and if you refuse to meet this need, she may continue to be a faithful wife, but her heart will ache for this expression. Instead, if you fill your wife's tank with repeated

---

29. Nonsexual Touching has already been addressed in Lesson 4.

deposits of Affection and Romance, it is like buying insurance that she won't seek attention from other men. Of course, *it is wrong* for her to want tingly excitement from other men, but I'm only telling you how fallen humans feel. *Affairs are about unmet emotional needs and women have an emotional need and desire to be romanced.* Any man who doesn't take the time and effort to learn this principle is a fool as the payoff is extremely rich—and the repercussions of not doing so are equally extreme."

If I don't massage her ego, she wants attention from other guys. Pathetic, just pathetic.

"Although the hormones that drove you to be romantic earlier are gone, you can still *choose* to romance her."

Some hormones, I've noticed, are still driving parts of my body.

"And don't forget that appropriate SUGs (Surprise and Unexpected Gifts) can communicate Affection and Romance as well.[30] Christina loved the wallet you gave her."

She did, but this whole Genie thing is costing too much.

"One of the easiest but most overlooked actions you can do to demonstrate Affection and Romance," he says, "is to simply look into her eyes and smile. It's staggering to know how few husbands have regular, sustained romantic eye contact with their wives."

Thinking about this, I realize how much eye contact I have with Delaney, and that pang of guilt fires through me.

"Know that Affection and Romance are important nutrients to add to your garden for a robust harvest. I am going to Jordan for a Dead Sea salt bath but will be back soon for Lesson 9," he says, and he's gone.

The Genie keeps harping on this idea that I'm to focus on how I love and give, not on how I'm loved and given to. How does any normal man do this in my intolerable situation?

Pulling my mind away from the Genie's unfair and false lecture, I walk into Rutherford's office. There are three other men in the conference room

---

30. SUGs are discussed in Lesson 3.

as well as Delaney. She immediately lights up when she sees me. She has on tight black leggings stuck in black leather boots, along with a long red shirt that almost covers her butt, but not quite. The top two buttons on her shirt are unbuttoned, allowing a sneak peek at her cleavage. Christina's fear alarm would rise to a deafening level if she were watching this scene on Facetime.

After shaking Rutherford's hand, I sit in the seat he assigns, next to Delaney.

"Jason, after looking at your proposal," he begins, "and discussing it thoroughly with Delaney and my associates, I am ready to seriously consider giving you the financial backing you want. Since I personally know how you transform not only a body but also a mind, I realize you have something unique to add to the world of fitness."

For Rutherford, that was a departure from his usual, cold demeanor. His positive response makes me think that maybe my gyms are going to be born right here, right now.

Glancing at Delaney, I sense she is ablaze with desire and encouragement. I wonder how I will ever make it through this business deal with Delaney's overt availability. I guess I'll think about that later.

Rutherford and his assistants all fire questions at me, which I am easily able to handle. Then turning to Rutherford, they all give him a thumbs up.

"We are prepared to offer you forty percent of the profits of this business venture," Rutherford says. "My associates are skilled in making business agreements that are highly conducive to both parties. We will draw up a contract and get back to you. As you know, Delaney and you will be working closely together to get our project up and running."

"Yes, sir," I say. "Thank you for this opportunity." Turning to Delaney to say a quick good-bye, I notice she is lit up like a Fourth of July fireworks display.

Thoughts of working long hours alone with Delaney prick my conscience, but quickly, I dismiss that negative thought, because I don't want anything to spoil this magic moment. Forty percent! Now we're talking!

Arriving home, I see Christina pull into the driveway, too. She is returning from taking dinner to her eighty-eight-year-old grandmother. After helping Christina get the kids inside, I tell her how Rutherford is going to fund the business and give me 40 percent of the profits. I can tell she is genuinely happy and proud of me. Intentionally, of course, while I was explaining the new arrangement to Christina, I left out the part about Delaney. Is it dishonest to leave out details like that?

Deciding it's not, I walk into my bedroom to change clothes. After all, this is business. And a man has to separate his business from his personal life, right?

SUMMARY OF LESSON 8

Understand Your Wife's Desire for Affection and Romance

Do...

... realize that although most men do not care about Affection and Romance, women never outgrow their desire for it.

... give tender words daily.

... realize that if you fail to give your wife Affection and Romance, she will want it from other men.

... give your wife plenty of Nonsexual Touching.

... look into her eyes and smile.

Don't...

... give Affection and Romance merely when you have a sexual urge, but try to give it at other times.

... think your wife is like the radical fringe who doesn't want her door opened.

... neglect giving your wife Affection and Romance just because the hormones driving it are gone. Choose to give it to her.

LESSON 9

Understand the Leadership
Style Your Wife Needs

Wednesday night, November 7

Although there is some improvement in my relationship with Christina, she still frequently criticizes and corrects[31] me, and I'm still not getting enough sex. In addition to this discouraging scenario, our anniversary is approaching, and I dread getting psyched up again to orchestrate the Big Five. We just celebrated her birthday. Is it really necessary for me to do all of that rigmarole again? Especially since I got her a SUG?

After Christina gets in bed—even though it's a colossal effort—I decide to love her in a language she can hear. First, I give her Admiration. I tell her how sweet and kind she is to her grandmother. While stroking her arm and looking into her eyes, I say, "Your concern for others is one of my favorite things about you." (I consider injecting that I'd like more concern in my direction but, of course, I don't.) Second, I rock the Big Five principle by making plans to go to Mia's Restaurant this Friday night for our anniversary.

---

31. If your wife frequently corrects and criticizes you, ask her to read *Wife School*, especially chapter 2 on Acceptance. (*Wife School Advanced* will be out in late 2017 and the two books together will open your wife's eyes to the respect and attention you want.)

After this heroic display, I mention sex, because after all, it's been nine days. She says she's tired, and our anniversary is only two days away, so how about then? After all my repeated efforts at Deep Conversation, Admiration and Appreciation, the Big Five, Household Help, and rocking Fatherhood, as well as the other annoying tenets, I'm *still* getting turned down. Maybe things are a little better, but these last two lessons had better be magic, because this partnership stills need a miracle. After the Genie teaches me the eleventh non-negotiable secret, I'm going to ask for the two main things I want: regular sex and for her to stop correcting and criticizing me. Naturally, I would also like her to praise me more, keep the house in better order, make my desires a higher priority, stay on the budget, and quit eating sugar and junky carbs so she can get back to the hot body she had before the kids. But I know to just ask for one (or two) things at a time. How I wish I could simply give her a list and tell her I will evaluate her performance in a couple of weeks!

Friday noon, November 9

After training three clients, I sit in my car and eat the lunch I packed for myself this morning. As I finish, I get a text from Delaney.

"I found a GREAT location for our first gym. It's perfect: Preston Hollow! Do you have any time today to meet me to look at it?"

Since I have a cancellation in my schedule right now, I text back: "I have 90 free minutes right now. I just finished training your dad."

She texts back: "Oh! I'm close to that location. I'll swing by and pick you up so we can talk about the renovation on the way there. See you in 5, okay?"

Even though I'm taken aback by the thought of riding in her sexy yellow Porsche Boxster alone with her, I agree. In five minutes, her Porsche arrives, and I get in. She has Beyoncé's album, Lemonade, playing, and the smell of her perfume fills the car. Her tight jeans are topped with a tight T-shirt, revealing a good look at her bulging breasts. That familiar surge in my body starts to churn.

While driving, Delaney dances a little to the music, and she playfully hits me in the chest, when I don't get one of her jokes. I should not be in this car.

As we walk around the location, we both realize how ideal it would be. But honestly, I am thinking more about how she looks in those jeans than I am about the square footage of the building. Her hair is thick and long, and I visualize how it would look, hanging down over…well…I realize I'm in a zone I should not be in. Warning sirens are blasting, but I'm not doing anything about them.[32]

Getting back in the car, she asks me if I mind if we quickly stop by her apartment on the way back as she needs to show me the specs she printed on the rental location. "It will only take a second," she says.

As dense as I am, even I know this is a setup. If I walk into her apartment, I'm not sure if I can resist. I'm at a crossroads. I want to give in. I do. I need to get out of here. I need to get out of here. I need to get out of here.[33]

My phone rings, and it's Christina. I consider not picking up, but since she usually texts instead of calling, I know I need to. "It's my wife," I say, hoping she will get the hint to stay quiet. She gets it and turns off the music.

Answering, I say, "What's up?"

---

32. "The prudent see danger and take refuge, but the simple keep going and pay the penalty" (Prov. 27:12).

33. "All at once he followed her like an ox going to the slaughter, like a deer stepping into a noose" (Prov. 7:22). When a man has an affair, it is extremely difficult for him to ever fully recover with his wife (of course, with God, all things are possible). Not only is a man's family ripped apart when he has an affair but he also loses credibility with his peers, his business associates, and his fellow church members. Having an affair is truly a fork in the road that can put your life in a different trajectory. The desire for the strange woman can be overwhelming, but if men knew the fallout they are going to pay, they would choose to be faithful. Just ask men who have made this mistake, and they will tell you that the hours of ecstasy with the strange woman were not worth the loss of respect from family, friends, community, business, etc. But most importantly of all, a man who strays is directly disobeying God.

"Mason jumped off the table again and this time, he cut his forehead right above his eyebrow. I'm sure he's going to need stitches. Can you meet me at the emergency room at Baylor Hospital downtown?" Her voice has the sound of mild terror.

"It will take forty-five minutes to get to Baylor in this traffic," I say. "Medical City Hospital is a lot closer for both of us."

Adamantly, Christina states she wants to go to Baylor because her Uncle TD is an ER doctor there, and he's working this shift. This is not a hill to die on so I agree to meet her there.

After Delaney drops me off, I head to Baylor. I'm not sure if that phone call was divine intervention or not, as there was the plump roast chicken before me, begging me to dine. How will I ever withstand this temptation during our upcoming business arrangement?

"You nearly hit a landmine in that girl's apartment," the Genie says, as he abruptly appears in my passenger seat.

"No, it wasn't dangerous," I lie, not willing to admit how close that one was.

Ignoring my comment, he begins, "Today we will discuss lesson nine, Understand the Leadership Style Your Wife Needs."

Sitting back, I surrender to listening to another unpleasant lesson.

"The two most common leadership styles of husbands are Commander Leadership and Passive Leadership. First we will discuss the Commander style."

The problem in our marriage is not with any leadership style. The problem is Christina's unwillingness to follow.

"A husband with a Commander style thinks that because he is the head in the marriage, his wife should comply with his orders. A man with this style also believes his happiness, his goals, and his concerns are more important than his wife's."

I might not say that out loud, but I do believe it.

"In the military, leadership consists of the higher-ranking officers giving orders to subordinates. Likewise in business, those in higher positions tell those in lesser positions what to do."

I like where this is going. Maybe this *Husband School* is finally onto something. Maybe I'm going to learn how to get Christina to do what I say and follow me. Cool.

"In ancient days, as you might know, the normal household codes were that men were to rule their wives, as if they were chattel or possessions," he continues. "Men felt like women were given to them, so they could enjoy more comfort and convenience in life."

Ha ha, yeah, the good ole days.

"But the Creator radically shocked His audience a couple thousand years ago, when He taught men some new principles regarding their marriage. The new teaching stated that in marriage, the man was to *care about his wife's welfare as much as his own*.[34] He was to sacrifice for her[35] and serve her.[36] The man was to make his wife the object of his love without her first being deserving of it.[37]

Uhhh…wait a second. What is this garbage?

"In the Creator's Word, children are told to obey.[38] Servants are told to obey.[39] Wives are told to submit.[40] This submission is a voluntary willingness of wives to put themselves under the leadership of their husbands. A wife's willing submission is *in response* to the relationship with her husband who woos and wins her.[41]

---

34. "In this same way, husbands ought to love their wives as their own bodies" (Eph. 5:28a)

35. "Husbands, love your wives, just as Christ loved the church and gave himself up for her" (Eph. 5:25).

36. "For even the Son of Man did not come to be served, but to serve…" (Mark 10:45).

37. "But God demonstrates his own love for us in this: While we were still sinners, Christ died for us" (Rom. 5:8).

38. Paul uses the Greek word *hypotasso* regarding children in Ephesians 6:1 and Colossians 3:20.

39. Paul again uses the Greek word *hypotasso* regarding servants in Ephesians 6:5 and Colossians 3:22.

40. Paul uses a different Greek word *hypakouo* regarding wives in Ephesians 5:24, Colossians 3:18, and Titus 2:5. Children and servants obey; wives voluntarily submit.

41. "We love because He first loved us" (1 John 4:19). In *Wife School*, we teach women their responsibilities, such as submitting without a husband first deserving it. In marriage, each spouse must focus on his or her own biblical responsibilities.

I'm not taking this malarkey. "Genie, the Creator's Word doesn't say man was created for woman, but woman for man." Get your facts right, man.

"Yes, the woman was created to be his completer, companion, and helper in fulfilling his call to be fruitful, multiply, and subdue the earth.[42] But many men like to think that a completer, companion, and helper means an enthusiastic sex partner, a cheerful housekeeper, and a personal butler. That is a gross misunderstanding of the reason the Creator made woman. The Creator's Word states that 'it is not good for the man to be alone,'[43] which speaks primarily of a companion, not a servant."

Could he be making this up?

"Men with the Commander Leadership style have a tendency to see their life as a wheel," he says. "The man sees himself as the center of that wheel, and each spoke represents a part of his life. There's the spoke of his job, the spoke of his hobbies, the spoke of his children, and the spoke of his wife, as well as many other spokes. A man usually sees all these spokes as belonging to him, as something he is in charge of and owns."

Not a bad analogy.

"But wives are not spokes. When two people marry, they become one.[44] She is now one half and you are one half of the whole. Since she is now fused with you, when you take care of her, you benefit yourself. However, the Commander style does not accept this responsibility to equally care for his wife as he cares for himself."

This Genie keeps preaching a ridiculous and impossible standard.

"The second common category of leadership styles is Passive Leadership," he says. "The husband with a Passive Leadership style realizes it is much more pleasant to think about work, money, sex, and hobbies than to enter the chaos of family life. This man chooses the path of least resistance and lets his wife run the family."

---

42. "Be fruitful and increase in number; fill the earth and subdue it" (Gen. 1:28).

43. "The LORD God said, "It is not good for the man to be alone. I will make a helper suitable for him" (Gen. 2:18).

44. "And the two will become one flesh" (Mark 10:8).

Anyone would agree it is easier to relax with a beer and a Cowboys football game than to get involved with Christina's mess.

"Passive Leadership husbands want to avoid conflict. This inattention and neglect, however, will make his wife feel unloved."[45]

Who can ever adequately love his wife by this numbskull's standards?

"In contrast to these two leadership styles, there is a third one, the Sacrificial/ Servant style. This leadership style of a husband considers the interests of his wife as important as his own."

No one does this![46]

"A husband who repeatedly exhibits a Sacrificial/Servant Leadership style will eventually have a wife who wants his highest good and happiness," he continues. "In addition, a woman who is well loved over time will learn to trust her husband and will not have as much difficulty submitting to his leadership. *It is the woman who does not trust her husband and who does not feel well loved that resists her call to submit.*"

The idea that some of Christina's past defiance may be my fault sharply stings for a moment, but I quickly dismiss that erroneous thought.

"A husband with a Sacrificial/Servant style doesn't demand that his wife follow because he holds the title and position of head," he continues. "Rather, *he earns the right to lead and influence* by humbly serving his wife."[47]

Isn't it time for this lesson to end?

"Even by the physical structures of a man's and a woman's body, it is obvious that a woman is to receive the man as in the sexual relationship," he says. "But even in this physical analogy, the woman is never forced, but coaxed and aroused with tenderness and attention to happily receive

---

45. Leadership in marriage is difficult because there is a delicate balance between overlooking the mistakes and weaknesses of your wife and the necessity of confronting a flagrant sin. If a prayerful man is filled with the Holy Spirit and walking with God, he can expect God to give him wisdom (see Prov. 3: 4–5).

46. No human does this well naturally, but a godly man can do this supernaturally.

47. All women have some trouble submitting, as it is a curse from the Garden of Eden (Gen. 3:16), but Christ has freed women from the curse (Gal. 3:13)! Your wife can read about the subject of authority in *Wife School*, chapter 9.

her husband. A woman who is treated with this tenderness and attention will also more easily receive her husband's direction and leadership. But the order is always that *the husband goes first*. Just like so many husbands want to have sex without the necessary warm-up of words and affection, some husbands want to give orders without consulting or considering a wife's viewpoint and wishes."

Is he now trying to connect Christina's sexual coldness with my failure to warm her up? Is there no end to his accusations?

"Your wife knows when her dreams, hopes, and goals are equal in your mind with yours," he says. "And conversely, she also knows when you see her as a mere aide to assist you in your journey. When your wife feels loved, respected, and valued, she is much more willing to follow you."

Maybe most women, but not Christina.

"A man who lacks a Sacrificial/Servant Leadership style will be inconsiderate of his wife," he says. "This man will not care if his wife becomes overheated while cooking in the kitchen, but only that he doesn't spend money on air conditioning. He will finish paying bills, even though his wife has called him to dinner. He will ignore his wife's desire to paint the outside of the house but instead, use the money to invest in the latest and greatest stock. This husband knows his wife is having company and wants him home early to help, but instead he stays at work and reads one more report or makes one more phone call."

I…uh…well…

"A man who lacks a Sacrificial/Servant Leadership style won't ask his wife's opinion before he plans a thousand dollar canoe trip to Canada with his buddies. This husband won't ask his wife's opinion before he signs up to play rec basketball twice a week or before he accepts a dinner date with his family of origin."

This is getting a little personal, since I contacted my college buddies last week about a canoe trip to Canada, and of course, without consulting Christina.

"Although unpopular decisions must sometimes be made by the husband for the ultimate good of your family, family members will ultimately understand over time that the heart of the Sacrificial/Servant Leadership style husband consistently has their good in mind instead of his own personal comfort or convenience."

He's got me in a corner, and he's pounding me with a right upper cut and then a short, straight jab. I feel like my eyes are swollen shut, I have lost a tooth, and I can barely breathe. I'm about to go down for the count.

"You don't lead by responding to how you're treated," he says. "You lead by doing what is right. Wise leaders overlook; they forgive; they don't keep a record of wrongs;[48] they return a blessing for an insult,"[49] the Genie says.

I've definitely not worked hard to love Christina to the extent that I love myself because I haven't thought she deserved it. But now I'm seeing another perspective, one that says *since I'm the leader, I go first.* I am to give without measuring how much I'm getting back.[50] The paradigm switch is mind-blowing.

"I'm going to Cairo for a massage, but I'll be back soon," the Genie concludes, swirls into smoke, and disappears.

As these lessons progress, I had hopes they would get easier, but that was a joke.

As I continue the drive toward Baylor, I realize that since I am the leader, how Christina treats me is not the main issue, *but how I treat her is.* I'm a little woozy thinking about it. My whole viewpoint of what it means to be the leader of my home[51] has been shattered. I have used my position

---

48. "[Love] does not dishonor others, it is not self-seeking, it is not easily angered, it keeps no record of wrongs" (1 Cor. 13:5).

49. "Do not repay evil with evil or insult with insult. On the contrary, repay evil with blessing, because to this you were called so that you may inherit a blessing" (1 Pet. 3: 9).

50. Jesus is the Vine and you are the branch (John 15:5). He can meet your needs and fill you with Himself, so you can meet your wife's needs without her first meeting yours.

51. When you follow Christ and when you demonstrate that you are a Sacrificial/ Servant Leader, then you can confidently ask your family to follow you. "Follow my example, as I follow the example of Christ" (1 Cor. 11:1).

of leadership for my own convenience and comfort instead of using it for the reason it was given to me, *to serve those entrusted to my care.* A conviction as heavy as the entire cosmos is pressing down on my chest.

I'm still not sure what to do about the business deal with Rutherford and his sexy daughter, but one thing I do know is that I'm *not* going to sleep with Delaney. If I get into a predicament in which my body screams for her, I will remember this moment and know that I will not abandon my marriage vows, no matter what, no matter what. I purpose to be a Sacrificial/Servant Leader in my marriage, from here on out.

Arriving at the Emergency Room, I immediately sense Christina's fear so I walk up and hug her. Uncle TD walks out to meet us and then guides us to a private room, with various nurses and techs shuffling in and out. Mason gets the treatment you might expect Princess Kate's son, Prince George, to get if he were getting stitches. Mason gets four stitches over his left eyebrow.

Tonight is our scheduled anniversary dinner at Mia's, but with all the intensity of the ER situation, I wasn't sure if Christina would still want to go. But she does. Thinking about my afternoon's earlier lesson with the Genie, I resolve that I will treat my wife in a manner that pleases the Creator. *It has nothing to do with Christina.* It only has to do with who the Creator wants *me* to be.

Reviewing all the steps to celebrate the Big Five, I think I have everything covered for the night. Flowers, check. Wrapped present (luckily, an inexpensive bracelet she has picked out), check. Mushy card, check. And now the last item on the list, dinner (and happily, this restaurant is not too pricey), check. Celebrating the Big Five is a big pain, but the Genie insists this is important to women.

As we drive to Mia's, Christina asks me to turn on the heater because she is chilly. "My heater is broken," I say. "I'm getting it fixed next week. The mechanic's estimate is $1200 but fortunately, we have that money set aside for automobile repairs."

Disappointment quickly registers on her face. "What's wrong?" I ask.

"I was going to ask you tonight if we could hire a cleaning service twice a month to help me, but with that expense, I'm sure there's no money."

Without further thinking, I already know what to say to her. "I don't like you to be tired or overworked. I've got a down jacket in my closet that keeps me warm even in subfreezing weather. I don't have to fix the heater right now. I'd rather get you some household help."

Turning to look at me, a big tear rolls down her cheek. "That is the sweetest thing I've ever heard, Jason. I can't believe you are going to go without heat in your car, so I can have household help."

I'm pretty shocked myself.

"Your happiness is important to me," I say, reaching over and patting her leg, giving her a dose of Nonsexual Touching. Christina puts her hand on top of mine and continues to look at me and smile.

Upon entering Mia's restaurant, the hostess leads us to our table. At the table next to us, I see Kevin White with his wife and four of their grandchildren. Introducing Christina, I explain to her that Kevin is the generous guy with whom I barter space. Kevin then proceeds to tell Christina what a "one-of-a-kind" trainer I am. I wish Christina would rave over me like this.

After we get seated, I notice a particular woman out of the corner of my eye. Looking more closely, I realize it is Delaney at the bar with a couple of her friends. Quickly I turn my face so she won't recognize me, but it's too late, and she walks over to our table. Her outfit—short shorts with a gypsy-looking, midriff-baring top—is absolutely ridiculous.

"Well," she purrs, "if it isn't my trainer and new business associate, Jason. Awesome to see you." She's slurring her words a little. I'm pretty certain she's tipsy. Hopefully she won't mention being together today.

One of her friends, who is also drunk, walks up to our table. "We've been hearing about Delaney's hot trainer for months and now, we hear you're going to work together. Delaney is beyond excited. If I sign you up as my trainer, can you get me a firm butt like Delaney's?" Both of them laugh hysterically.

Looking at Christina, I notice her eyeballs are the size of golf balls. "Christina, this is Delaney, Rutherford's daughter."

"Hello, Wife," she slurs. "Jason doesn't wear a ring, but he did say he had a wife." Christina's eyes now go from the size of golf balls to tennis balls.

Turning to Christina, I say, "My wedding ring gives me a blister when I lift weights. I have always taken off my wedding ring while I train clients."

Christina is still looking at me in shock. Ignoring the two drunk girls, I continue talking to Christina, "I also don't wear a ring when I play golf because it gives me a blister. But I wear my ring every other second except when I'm playing sports." And that's the truth.

After the girls walk away, Christina, who is visibly upset, asks me, "What does she mean, 'you are her new business associate'?"

"That's Rutherford's daughter," I say. "She's in charge of her father's new business ventures, so I will be working with her to open the gyms."

"Jason," she says, with utter exasperation, "you've got to be kidding me. That screams danger in every direction. That woman is crazy about you! Surely there is someone else in this huge city of Dallas you can find to fund your gyms besides her father."

Although I'm upset thinking about finding someone else to fund my gyms, at the same time I know that Christina is right about the risk of working with Delaney. But where would I ever find someone else who would give me 40 percent of the profits?

"Jason," Christina continues, "I cannot tell you how upset I am that you will be working with her. I would rather us struggle forever financially than for you to work with her. Please get out of it."

The problem is, *I'm* not willing to struggle forever financially.

"Why didn't you tell me you were working with Rutherford's daughter? You didn't tell me because you knew I wouldn't like it. Something is wrong, Jason, and you know it. We have three children and a marriage to take care of. I hope you haven't already cheated on me because that would devastate me."

"Christina, I promise I haven't cheated on you."

Of course, I don't tell her how *I almost did...*and how I, too, am concerned about how I can withstand the temptation once I begin to be alone all the time with the plump roast chicken.

"I can't even imagine how horrible it would be for me, knowing you are working with her every day. I need to go home now. I can't sit here any longer." We haven't even ordered, but she gets up to walk toward the door. Some anniversary dinner.

"Jason," Delaney says loudly across the restaurant, "See you Monday." She and her friends start giggling again.

"Bye, Mr. Hot Trainer," one of her drunk friends adds.

Walking out of the restaurant, Christina can't even talk. We drive home in silence and when we pull into the garage, she looks me squarely in the eyes. "I absolutely *cannot* take it if you work with her. I don't even like it that you train her. Something is very wrong, Jason." She gets out of the car and stomps into the house. I follow her, pay the babysitter, and then head to the bedroom. I've had about enough of her stuff.

I say, "You know what, Christina? You need to grow up. I'm trying to support you and all these blooming kids and then you act like a child, stomping out of the restaurant. Why can't you act like an adult?"

She slams the bedroom door, and I can hear the click of the lock.

Through the locked door, I yell, "Why don't you carry the financial load of the family? Huh? You want another child, new bedroom furniture, private education, and then when I almost land a business deal so I can pay for all of your crap, you want me to get out of it. So why don't you support this family, Christina? Huh? Huh?"

There is silence on the other side of the door, so I head to the den to try to get comfortable on the couch. Maybe I shouldn't have said all of that, but I get sick of carrying this family's financial load without more support, and without more sex!

Even after giving up a heater in my car for the winter, I'm still in the doghouse.

SUMMARY OF LESSON 9

Understand the Leadership Style Your Wife Needs

Do...

> . . . remember that a Sacrificial/Servant Leadership style husband cares about his wife's welfare as much as his own.

> . . . realize that a wife who is well loved over time will not have as much difficulty submitting to his leadership.

> . . . earn the right to lead by humbly serving your wife.

> . . . remember that wise leaders overlook, forgive, don't keep a record of wrongs, and return a blessing for insult.

> . . . remember that since you're the leader, you go first.

Don't...

> . . . expect your wife to submit just because of your position of head, without first loving her well.

> . . . be inconsiderate of your wife's dreams, hopes, goals, and comfort.

LESSON 10

Understand How Anger and Harsh Words Affect Your Wife

Tuesday, November 13

Christina and I have barely spoken since the restaurant fiasco last Friday night, and I feel that all-too-familiar chill between us.

Delaney changed her usual session from 4:00 p.m. to 11:00 a.m. because of a hair appointment. Opening the door to her father's workout room, I see she is already there, warming up on the treadmill, with her usual bare-minimum outfit. I guess now is as good a time as any to have this conversation. Diving right in, I begin, "Delaney, my wife is unhappy with me working so closely with you in our new business."

She laughs as if that's the most ridiculous thing she's ever heard. "Did you tell her you wear the pants in the family, and you'll work with who you want to work with?" Her face is lit with energy and confidence.

"Uh, no, I didn't quite say that."

"What did you say, 'Mr. Hot Trainer'?" she says as she laughs, obviously quoting her friend from the other night. She's stretching and leaning over, exposing too much as usual.

This is harder than I thought it would be, but I continue, "To make Christina happy, I'm afraid I'm going to have to back out of our business deal."

"*What?*" she almost screams. "After my dad agreed to fund you, you're going to back out? Just because your wife doesn't want you working with me?"

"Uh, well, I'm sorry." I can feel the sweat beading up on my forehead.

"Look, Jason," she says, as she walks toward me in her short purple workout shorts, "what goes on between you and me is our business. Your wife doesn't need to know." We stare at each other, and that wild, sexual craziness starts to take over my body. She steps even closer and puts her hands on my shoulders.

The trifold effect of having her breasts thrust in my face, her availability, and the privacy of the room causes me to want to rethink my decision. But with what little resolve I can muster, I will myself to remember my vow to the Creator. Being an adulterer is not the person I want to be when I'm in my sane mind, *which is not now*. I've got to get away from this woman who hijacks every sinew in my body.

Stepping back from Delaney, I look down. By this gesture, she knows that I am saying no, and she steps back also.

"I want to keep my marriage," I say.

"Buddy, you're missing a lot of fun," she says. "And you're going to have to tell my dad, not me."

Thoughts of telling Rutherford make me feel even more anxious. Delaney calls her father and he's free, so we walk upstairs to his office on the sixth floor.

Entering the office, I explain everything to Rutherford. "It's insulting, Jason, that you think my daughter would even be interested in you. If you ever want to be successful, you're going to have to learn to separate business and personal life. I think I'll find another trainer, as well. It would be uncomfortable for all of us in the future. Now, if you'll excuse me, I have other business to attend to." He motions with both hands for me to leave.

Walking out of Rutherford's high rise, I feel torn. Although I'm sick I'm walking away from the funding of my gyms, I feel peaceful because I know I did the right thing. Working with Delaney was a temptation too dangerous for me. As much as I craved her, I know that sleeping with her and breaking my marriage vows would have damaged my marriage and life forever. I avoided that landmine, but only by a whisker.

Driving to my next appointment, the Genie again appears in my passenger seat.

"Nice work, getting out of that business deal," the Genie says. "I'm proud of you for realizing how dangerous that young woman was and how she might have wrecked your marriage beyond repair."[52]

The thought of losing the arrangement with 40 percent profit pricks me again. And in addition, these lessons make me feel like I'm an orange being racked on the juicer.

"Our important topic today is Understand How Anger and Harsh Words Affect Your Wife," he announces.

I knew I shouldn't have unloaded on Christina last Friday night.

"If you are in an elevator, and someone accidentally bumps into you, it is no big deal," the Genie says. "But if you are in an elevator and you're sunburned, and someone bumps into you, it hurts. A wife has a sensitivity to her husband's remarks like a person with a sunburn has a sensitivity to a bump. Therefore, you must speak to your wife knowing she is created this way. You cannot rip off a few coarse words, just because you're angry or annoyed."

I bet he watched me yell at Christina through the bedroom door the other night.

"Of course, your wife is going to be upset with you," he says. "And when she does, your natural tendency is to straighten her out with a strong, angry tone. You raise your voice in order to enlighten her to what she should or should not have done."

"Genie, that's how humans let other humans know when they're upset," I say, hoping to get a pass for my Friday night fury.

---

52. God is still in the business of performing miracles. "Now to Him who is able to do exceedingly abundantly above all that we ask or think, according to the power that works in us..." (Eph. 3:20).

"That's how *immature* humans let others know they're upset," he says. "*Mature* people don't use negative voice tones because they are offended or annoyed. You can communicate that you don't like the other one's choices without using harshness, disrespect, or volume. In fact, the way couples speak to each other when they disagree reveals a lot about the health of their marriage."

I think he's trying to say I'm immature.

"Husbands think they get to let down at home and act how they feel, since they have been using self-control all day at work. But this is a huge error. Uncontrolled and improper words said to your wife can have disastrous consequences that can take weeks—if not months—to recover from."

We have certainly not recovered from Friday night.

"Self-control is always the virtue," he says, "as opposed to giving in to your natural inclinations. Your mind set should be to save your best relationship skills for marriage."

In the past, I would've said that saving your best for marriage was ridiculous, but maybe what is ridiculous is that I've *not* realized this.

"A wife retreats and builds walls when faced with the anger and harshness of her husband," he says. "She is not built to handle this negative behavior from her husband."

"But she was wrong and immature to stomp out of Mia's last Friday night," I plead.

"Remember how wise leaders live," he says. "They focus on how they love and give; they overlook; they forgive; they don't keep a record of wrongs; they return a blessing for insult,"[53] the Genie says.

Guess there's still a learning curve for me with the Leadership lesson.

"What is comical to me, Young Jason, is how men are attracted to and marry women with opposite personalities but then are upset when their

---

53. Maybe this behavior is rare to witness, but actually, it is merely how the Christian is called to live. "Do not repay evil with evil or insult with insult. On the contrary, repay evil with blessing..." (1 Pet. 3:9).

wife is not more like them! For example, a man values his wife's calm, introverted spirit but then complains she does not want to go out and be as social as he wants. Another man is initially attracted to his wife's lively and extraverted personality but is then annoyed by her lack of attention to detail. All wives have a weakness set, just like all husbands, because they are human. You must learn to accept the weakness set your wife brings to your marriage. When your wife behaves in a manner unlike the way you would respond, remember that difference is part of the reason you were attracted to her in the first place."

I hadn't thought about how *all* people have weaknesses, so therefore, of course, Christina has some.

"Another concept to embrace that helps husbands is to invoke the Forty-eight Hour Rule when you are annoyed or irritated with Christina."

I'm too old for all of these cheesy names.

"A very wise yet infrequent strategy in marriage is to wait forty-eight hours before you speak to Christina about an offense. If her offense is large—such as if she spends a substantial amount of money without consulting you—then you will have sufficiently calmed down after forty-eight hours, so you can speak to her rationally and without anger."

Memories of when Christina bought a $150 membership to a kids' indoor playground without consulting me returns. I was so mad I didn't even wait forty-eight seconds to confront her.

"The Forty-eight Hour Rule will eliminate firing off critical remarks in the passion of the moment and can eliminate spouses saying hurt-ful things they later regret," he says. "This rule alone can prevent much conflict."

The Forty-eight Hour Rule would have saved me from last Friday night's remarks.

"Another imperative and crucial element to understand is that when you hurt your wife with your anger, you *must* ask forgiveness. Men hope the conflict will fade away, and they won't have to apologize. But it doesn't. On the contrary, *conflict accumulates,* that is, unless you ask forgiveness."

No wonder he saved this lesson for last. Asking forgiveness is the worst! The absolute worst!

"Learn to say, 'I know I raised my voice, and I shouldn't have. You are the most important person in the world to me, and I didn't treat you with respect. Will you please forgive me?'"

Trying to get this intense spotlight off me, I ask, "Genie, what do I do if Christina escalates into emotional turmoil and is disrespectful to me?"

"If Christina escalates, it is imperative that you consistently control your own tone and volume. If you control your tone and volume, then most likely, she will simmer down in response.[54] If she does not, you can say, 'Christina, we're both upset. Let's table this conversation until we have both calmed down.'"

It's a stretch that I could say that, but I will try.

"In fact, men are stunned to learn that the overall ratio of positive to negative comments to his wife should be twenty-five to one," he says.[55]

"Genie, that is a ridiculous ratio," I say, thinking about a radio program I heard once that suggested a seven to one ratio.

"It is not ridiculous at all," he says. "Thriving interpersonal relationships only exist in a safe and positive culture. Humans flourish in environments of praise and wilt in environments of criticism and anger," he says.

I don't think I'll hit a twenty-five to one ratio, but I could certainly improve the current one.

"I will return soon," and he vaporizes into his usual hurricane of smoke and disappears.

Almost arriving at my next appointment, I realize I still have time to call Christina. She picks up on the first ring. Her voice is cool and detached. "Hello," she says.

"Christina, I want to ask you to forgive me for how I yelled at you the other night after Mia's. I was upset over you wanting me to get out of the

---

54. "A gentle answer turns away wrath, but a harsh word stirs up anger" (Prov. 15:1).
55. There are many opinions about the proper ratio. This is the one we like.

Rutherford deal, but I should have never talked to you so disrespectfully. I know I was wrong, and I'm going to try to treat you with the respect and honor you deserve. Will you please forgive me?"

Her voice softens a little, "Yes, I'll forgive you. I appreciate you apologizing."

There are a few moments of silence, and then I continue. "And guess what? I did it," I inform her.

"You did what?" she asks, still in a flat tone.

"I got out of the business deal with Rutherford. And in addition to that, I'm not training Rutherford or Delaney anymore." My voice sounds a lot chirpier than I really feel. I just gave up an unbelievable business opportunity.

Now Christina's voice has a *complete* change of tone. "Jason," she says in an excited and sweet voice, "I can't tell you what this means to me! I will never forget this. This is a huge gift. I know what a sacrifice it was for you to give up this deal, but it tells me how much you value our marriage."

"I knew it was the right thing to do," I say. "Our marriage is important to me."

There is a moment of silence on the phone, but I know I just added a large heap of nutrients to my garden.

"There's a big change in you, Jason. I'm not exactly sure what's happened, but you're different. It gives me a brand new affection for you."

Not sex, just affection.

"I realize I've not been the husband you've needed, and I'm determined to change," I say.

I can tell she is crying a little bit. "It's a very happy moment for me, Jason."

"I want you to be happy, Christina."

After staying on the phone in silence another twenty seconds, Christina says, "I know you need to get back to work. Thank you so much for taking your time to call me and tell me this."

"Okay, sweetheart," I say. "I'll see you tonight."

I have not called her sweetheart since the early days of the marriage. It wasn't even that hard to choke out, and I'm sure I got some points for supplying Affection and Romance.

Pulling into the parking lot of my next appointment, Christina texts me: "Britney Omar just texted me and asked for your contact information for her husband, Pete, a.k.a. Tower. Just FYI."

What does Tower want? Probably to thank me for calling Brent to look at his daughter's broken foot. I guess Christina had no choice but to give Britney my contact information.

Immediately, my text message lights up again. "Hey, Jason. This is Pete Omar. I was wondering if you could meet for coffee. I have something I want to discuss with you."

I have no interest in discussing anything with him. I type: "Maybe next week. I've got a lot going on right now," and right before I hit Send, I get another text message from Christina.

"I know you don't like Pete, but would you please try to be polite? Britney has always been one of my good friends."

I was just about to blow off the idiot. Now Christina is going to ask me what I said and what I did. I guess I could have coffee with the bum, thinking how it would please Christina. I delete what I just wrote to Tower and instead, text back: "I have a break today between three and four. Would that work for you?"

"Yes, what about the Starbucks in Preston Hollow?" he responds.

"OK, see you at 3," I reply.

I mean, how horrible could it be, for one hour?

At three o'clock, I walk into Starbucks, and Tower is already there. "Hey, Jason," he says as he stands to greet me and shake my hand. I think that is the first time he has ever called me Jason instead of the usual *Little Guy*.

After we get coffee, he jumps right in. "Jason, I want to apologize for not being friendlier to you. Even when I was rude to you on the soccer field, you still chose to help me with my daughter's broken foot. That showed me what kind of person you are."

Ooooookay, where is he going with this?

"Anyway, will you please accept my apology?"

What is my choice? I will accept it, but I certainly know that after a snake bites me once, I will keep my distance from that snake in the future.

"Apology accepted," I say, wondering how many more minutes until I can leave. This ogre wants to waste my time to ask me to forgive him?

"Now I will get to the reason I asked you to meet me today," he says. "As you might know, Pump It Up Gyms just opened their ninth location."

I had no idea. This guy much be filthy rich.

"I need a man that knows what he's doing in the gym as well as someone who knows how to handle himself. I would like to offer you a position," he says.

I can't believe this louse is offering me a job. I guess he wants me to clean bathrooms and wipe down the equipment. There's no way I'd take this job, no matter how much he offers me.

"I'd like to offer you the position of vice-president in which you'll be over all nine of the gyms. The starting salary is $200,000, but then you will also be subject to bonuses and raises."

Did he say $200K? Since I don't have any funding in sight for my gyms, maybe I should consider this. It's twice what I'm making now.

"So what do you think?" he asks.

"That's a very generous offer, Pete," I say. "Tell me more about the job." Pete proceeds to discuss the particular duties, all of which I would enjoy.

"Let me take a couple days to think about it," I say. I really don't need more than a couple days. I think the answer is going to be yes. Even though I can't stand the guy, that's a lot of money, and I need to save for the kids' college tuition. And I know, Christina will love this.

"Sure," he says, with a complete change from Dr. Jekyll to Mr. Hyde. "We will hammer out the details of the agreement, but I first wanted to see if you were open to it." What a different demeanor he now has since he wants something from me. I'm not too keen on working for such a jerk, but the money! The money! A ton of financial pressure would be lifted from me. This is certainly not how I predicted things would turn out, but wow, $200K!

SUMMARY OF LESSON 10

Understand How Anger and Harsh Words Affect Your Wife

Do...

> . . . realize your wife is easily wounded by your anger and harsh words.

> . . . remember that self-control—not giving in to your natural inclinations—is always the virtue.

> . . . accept your wife's weakness set.

> . . . enforce the Forty-eight Hour Rule when you are upset with your wife.

> . . . learn how to ask forgiveness.

> . . . aim for a twenty-five to one ratio of positive to negative comments with your wife.

Don't...

> . . . use harshness, disrespect, or increased volume when talking to your wife.

LESSON 11

Understand Your Wife's Desire for the One Thing

Still Tuesday, November 13

Driving home, I think about the earlier Genie lesson on Household Management, so I text Christina: "Do you want me to stop at the grocery store and pick anything up for you?"

She texts back: "That would be incredibly helpful! I have nothing to send Isabella in her lunch tomorrow. Could you please get cheddar cheese, nuts, and grapes? Thank You! Xoxo!"

The thought that Christina should plan better and have her shopping done runs through my mind, but I remember, *focus on how you love and give, not on how you are loved and given to.*

Just for fun, I decide to set my stop watch and see how long it takes me to park the car, get three grocery items, and get back in my car.

Okay, it took nine minutes. Nine minutes! I can do things like this without it costing me too much time or energy. And the Genie says this kind of attention pays off richly with wives.

Walking into the kitchen, Christina turns and smiles. She walks over to me and gives me a hello kiss. The children are bouncing off the walls as usual, but an affectionate wife covers a multitude of madness.

First, I ask Christina about her day, attempting to give her Deep

Conversation by Hitting the Ping Pong Ball Back. While I'm in the kitchen and she's talking, I start putting dishes in the dishwasher, as the Genie taught me that women adore help with household tasks. The kids are jumping on me, and I tell them that after dinner, we are going to play Flashlight Hide and Seek, their favorite game. Christina smiles as she watches me rock Fatherhood.

Quickly I change clothes and come back in the kitchen. During dinner, I give Christina a combined dose of Admiration, Affection, and Romance: "This is delicious salmon. A good-looking woman who can cook; now that's a deal." While looking into her eyes, I smile, and then reach over and squeeze her hand, giving her a Nonsexual Touch.

"Mommy makes great PBJ's, too. My lunch is good every day," Isabella adds as she smiles adoringly at her mother.

Christina looks like an eighteenth century painting, so content and peaceful. I can't believe this is the same woman that lived in this house a few weeks ago. These Genie secrets really do have magic in them.

Dinner is over, and I help carry dishes to the sink. I'll never get over hating doing dishes, but again, it's only eight to nine minutes. I can do that.

"What did Pete Omar want?" Christina asks.

"I've been excited to tell you," I say. "He wants me to be vice-president of his company and over all nine of his gyms. He offered me $200,000 to start out."

With her eyes on fire, she turns to look at me. "$200,000? Wow! That is a huge amount of money!"

"I know," I say. I knew she would love this.

"But you don't like Pete Omar, Jason. And what you really want is to find funding, so you can have your own line of gyms."

I'm shocked to hear her say this. Stunned.

"I'm surprised, Christina. I thought you would love for me to make that kind of money."

"I don't think you're going to be happy working for Pete Omar. Actually, he's not your caliber of person. And I know you have this dream of building your own line of gyms. I don't want you to give up pursuing the funding. Someone is going to recognize your greatness and want to help you." She smiles and adds, "That is, I want you to find funding without a Victoria's Secret supermodel attached."

I'm glad she doesn't know how close I got to that plump roast chicken.

Staring at Christina, it seems like somebody got into this woman's brain and erased and replaced the previous hard drive. She's telling me that someone's going to recognize my greatness? She's willing for me not to take that job so my happiness, goals, and dreams will be met? Is this really happening?

Walking over to her, I put my arms around her waist, look into her eyes, and gently push her hair off her forehead. "Thank you for supporting me in chasing my dream," I say as I sweetly kiss her forehead, a combination of Appreciation, Affection, and Romance. "Every man should have a beautiful, supportive wife like you."

She is giddy beyond belief. The happiness and sweetness all over her face are similar to the happiness and sweetness of the first time I met her in the cafeteria. We are having a moment, right here in the middle of soapy water, dishes, and wild kids.

I don't mention it and she doesn't either, but we both know we are going to have sex tonight. I kiss her forehead again and smile at her. I would like to grab her butt, but I know she mainly wants Nonsexual Touching. (Honestly, I only like the sexual kind of touching, but I am learning to give Christina love in a language she can hear.)

Maybe the Genie is not such a bozo after all.

After the kids are in bed, I shower and then Christina gets in the bathtub. As I do every night, I meander into the kitchen to be sure all the doors are locked. As I check the door to the garage, I notice the Genie is sitting on the washing machine in the laundry room. "What are you doing here?" I ask. "Christina is in the bathtub."

"She usually soaks for at least twenty minutes, which is much more time than I need for tonight's lesson. The topic tonight is Understand Your Wife's Desire for the One Thing."

What could he possibly say that he's not already said?

"We have previously discussed the mystique of women, how they are multi-faceted and multi-layered, while in contrast, men are usually much simpler."

Go on, I'm listening.

"In addition to the ten tenets that I've already taught you in *Husband School*, women will also have the One Thing she wants from you."

"How is a guy supposed to know what her sacred One Thing is?" I sarcastically inquire.

"Oh, men know," he says smiling. "*It's the thing she asks you for all the time, the thing you don't want to give.* One woman wants her husband to be more involved with her family of origin. Another woman wants her husband to be more engaged with the kids, so she can work. A third woman wants to find money to send the kids to private school while still another wife wants her husband to be home more with the family."

Christina repeatedly presses me for a fourth child. We can't handle three; why would we ever consider having a fourth?

"Genie, surely women don't get to rule the roost like this and tell their husbands what to do!"

"No," he laughs, "of course women don't get to tell men what to do, but when a wife has a *strong recurring theme of something she wants*, you have to deal with it—*not ignore it.* You have to acknowledge her unmet desire, that is, the One Thing. Discuss it, and then try to resolve or negotiate the issue."

Ignoring has definitely been my go-to strategy.

"Whether women want your time, your assistance, your support, or your money, they know if it is in your ability to give it to them," he says. "Wives don't usually press husbands for things that her husband *doesn't have an ability to give.* But they often press husbands for something husbands don't *want* to give."

"Genie, are you telling me to let Christina have another baby?"

"I'm definitely *not* telling you what to do about that," he says. "I'm only telling you that you must address her unmet desire, the One Thing, and *not ignore it*—which is the normal tendency of men. Discuss it, negotiate it, *and at least move toward her with an effort to problem solve.* She must sense that you care and are working toward a solution."[56]

Another pregnancy is out.

"Other typical responses of husbands when their wife asks for something they don't want to give is to belittle her, speak disrespectfully to her, be annoyed, be impatient, or be condescending."

I know those responses. I've used them many times when Christina brings up the baby issue.

"Wives expect to accommodate husbands all the time, and don't think much about it. But when husbands have to accommodate their wife, they think their rights are being infringed upon."

"She'll just keep asking me for more if I give her the One Thing," I say.

"Husbands like to say that, but most women will actually be satisfied and grateful if you move toward them with the One Thing. Talk through what she wants in a soft voice and try to move toward what she wants *in some way.* This is nothing more than simple negotiation."

Christina wants that fourth child, and she wants private education. Maybe if she agreed to homeschool, or to go to public school, I would consider it, because honestly, it's the financial strain that makes me not want to have any more kids. Negotiating is not a bad idea.

Returning to the bedroom after the Genie leaves, I realize Christina is still not out of the bathtub. So while waiting for her, I carefully scrub out my mouth (remembering the lesson about sex and hygiene). Then we get in bed and turn off the lights. We begin to make love, and Christina is much more engaged than usual. I work hard to carefully round the bases, talking to her about how desirable she is (working hard on her brain, her sex organ).

Bingo. I light up the pinball machine.

Afterward, I say, "Christina, I loved that."

"I enjoyed it, too," she says, and I can tell she means it.

---

56. Couples need to pray together about areas of conflict and ask God to show them His will.

"I can't quite express what it means to me to have sex like that," I say. "That was a ten out of ten for me."

Smiling again, she says, "Jason, you have been such a different person lately. What has happened to you?"

"I decided to focus on your needs," I say. "And in the meantime, I've realized again how beautiful and smart you are. And I can't tell you how supported I feel about my career. Very few wives would turn down a sure $200,000 to chase a husband's dream."

"So you're happy in our marriage?" she asks.

Uhhh...what do I say?

"Well, there is one thing I would like," I say. My palms are sweaty.

"What?" she asks, looking like a frightened teenager.

"I would like more of what just happened, Christina. Sex. I loved that. Just reveled in it. I cannot quite tell you what it means to me to have such a luscious wife to make love to. If I could have more frequent and regular sex, I'd be the happiest man in the world." Well, if she would quit criticizing me too, but actually, thinking about that now, she has not said anything negative for a few days.

"What is regular and frequent?" she asks.

I'm not sure what to say, so I ignore the question and ask her one. "How often would you like to have sex?"

"Probably every ten days to two weeks. How about you?" she asks.

I'm not shocked by her answer, but of course, I'm disappointed. "For me, it would be three to four times a week." Her eyebrows shoot up. Oh no, she is getting ready to scream, *"Jason, you're a dog in heat."*

Looking at the floor, she doesn't say anything.

"Do you think we could negotiate something in between?" I ask. "It would mean so much to me." I feel like a little puppy on his hind legs, begging for a biscuit.

"Oh my," she says. "I had no idea you felt so frustrated with our sex life."

What? She's thinking about *me* being frustrated? Is she saying that she feels bad about not giving me what *I* need? Is this possible?

Again, we just look at each other.

"I guess we could try twice a week," she says. "I know that's not nearly enough in your opinion—"

I jump in and interrupt.

"Honestly, twice a week would be amazing. Twice a week? That I could count on? That would be simply awesome."

Again, we look at each other and don't talk.

Breaking the silence, I say, "I've heard about some couples who schedule[57] when they have sex. In other words, they pick a couple of times each week they know they will have—"

This time, she interrupts.

"That would be a great relief to me, so I don't have to play this game with you of 'Can We Tonight?' If I knew what days and when, it would help me guard that time, so I could emotionally and physically prepare. When would you like to schedule?"

I can't believe this is happening.

We decide on Wednesday nights and Sunday afternoons after church during the kids' naptime. I walk over to Christina and put my arms around her and hold her. She starts breaking down into sobs.

Oh no. She's upset because she has to have sex with me twice a week. "What's wrong?" I ask.

"I can't remember the last time you came over and just put your arms around me to hold me and didn't want anything," she said. She is still crying.

I thought I just did that in the kitchen earlier tonight. Well, anyway, I hold Christina a little longer while she continues to sob.

"I'm crying because I'm so happy," she says. Again, we look at each other, and I realize that I have not been this happy myself in a long, long time.

---

57. Many couples could not conceive of scheduling sex, as it would take the spontaneity out of it. But couples who have a large discrepancy in their sexual appetites, as well as couples who are crazy busy, immensely benefit from scheduling and protecting time for sex. Each couple has to decide what works best for them.

SUMMARY OF LESSON 11

Understand Your Wife's Desire for the One Thing

Do...

> . . . realize that you have to acknowledge your wife's One Thing, trying to resolve or negotiate it, versus ignoring it.

Don't...

> . . . belittle, talk disrespectfully to her, be annoyed, impatient, or condescending over the One Thing.

CONCLUSION

Understand That Husbands—Not Wives— Are the Game Changers in Marriage

Wednesday, November 26

Although I don't have funding for my gyms, what a difference a happy wife makes. Christina corrected me this morning about how I was feeding the baby, but since I've asked for regular and more frequent sex, I've decided to wait awhile before I ask for anything else.

It's late Wednesday afternoon, and I'm at my gym for the last appointment of the week. Tomorrow is Thanksgiving, and I'm taking four days off. Kevin White, my landlord, will be here shortly for his workout. Waiting on Kevin, I notice the Genie's empty lantern in the corner, and I remember that he has not said goodbye.

Kevin arrives, and even with an intense workout, he sails through. He is more fit than most fifty-year-olds, but the lines in his face still give away his seventy years.

After our workout, I begin wiping down the equipment for the long holiday ahead. Kevin interrupts my train of thought. "Everything all right with you, Jason? You seem concerned about something."

Turning around, I reply, "That's funny you would notice. I almost landed a new business deal to open a line of gyms, and it recently fell through. So I guess I am kind of discouraged. Thanks for asking."

"Why did it fall through?"

Normally I'm relatively private, but for some reason, I want to talk about it. "I would have been working closely with a *very* attractive twenty-six-year-old, and when my wife met her, she fell apart. So actually, I turned down the deal to keep my marriage from imploding."

"Was your wife right? Was the twenty-six-year-old treacherous gear?"

"Highly hazardous," I say, smiling. Kevin's expression tells me he obviously understands the universal struggle men have to undergo to be monogamous.

"Even though I knew she was trouble," I continue, "I still had a hard time walking away because I was going to own forty percent of that business. However, I finally walked away, and now I'm without financial backing." I continue wiping down the elliptical.

"By chance, was it the young woman that was at Mia's the other night?" Kevin asks. I had completely forgotten that Kevin was at a nearby table when that whole drama went down.

"You got her," I say.

"I noticed you left without eating. I wondered if that young woman had something to do with it," he says.

"Her father was my financier, and she was in charge of supervising her father's new business acquisitions," I explain. Kevin shakes his head, communicating that he completely understands the entire scenario without me telling him anything more.

Changing the subject, he asks, "What kind of gyms do you want to open?"

He seems genuinely interested, so I proceed to tell Kevin a little about my goal of building a unique line of gyms that will teach people how to train their minds as well as their biceps. I know, however, that Buick-driving, Holiday Inn-staying Kevin is not the kind of guy who could ever finance something as colossal as my dream.

"Jason, it's an amazing concept you've got, and I know it works. Why, look how you've changed my life by teaching me about sugar, bad carbs, and exercise. Do you have any free time soon when you could show me your numbers and plans? I'm looking for an investment, and I like to invest in people I like. I doubly respect how you honored your marriage and walked away from that jeopardous situation."

If he knew how close I was to caving, he would never say that. The truth is that I was moments away from my demise.

"Are you busy now?" I ask. "My paperwork is in my trunk."

"Go get it," he says.

Outside, I text Christina and explain the situation. She writes back to take as long as I need.

Returning quickly, we spread the papers across the floor of the gym. He carefully pours over the numbers, like he's looking through a microscope. We don't talk for nearly twenty minutes.

"Jason, at first glance, this is a go for me. I like your predictions, your ideas, and of course, I'm really interested in investing in you, the man. I'll run all these numbers by my accountant to get his opinion, and then I'll get back to you. By the way, I usually like to offer my business partners fifty-one percent ownership in a project like this."

Stunned, I ask, "How can you be that generous?"

"I have found that entrepreneurs need to have the controlling interest in order to be motivated," he says. "People work harder when they are the majority stockholder. But then, I'll make more money, too. It's a win-win. And again, I like you and trust you. I would enjoy spending time with you, growing our business."

Fifty-one percent? Did I really hear him right? It all seems too good to be true. Kevin leaves, and as I start locking up, I realize that in a strange way, my funding found me.

Right before I exit, the Genie appears in the chair by my desk. "Kevin White is a trustworthy man," he begins. "I'm happy for you, Young Jason."

Staring at him a moment, I wonder if he poured any of his Genie pixie dust on Kevin White but decide he didn't.

"Although we have finished discussing the eleven non-negotiable tenets," he says, "I have one more thought that I want to leave with you. The topic is Understand That Husbands—Not Wives—Are the Game Changers in Marriage."

I was floating on a cloud five seconds ago, but now, I'm annoyed. "What is that supposed to mean?" I ask. Any previous contrite, humble mindset has now vanished. "Aren't wives responsible too? Calling me the Game Changer makes it seem like I'm the one responsible for this marriage, and that's unfair."

"Like it or not, it is still true that husbands largely determine the quality of a marriage," he replies.

With a tone that is much more civil than I feel, I ask, "Can you explain why I'm the Game Changer?" I'm willing to work on these eleven tenets, but he should be more reasonable and realize she is still responsible for her 50 percent of this marriage.

"I'll explain," he says smiling, as if he's got four aces in his poker hand. "Remember, on the shelf of your mind, you primarily have four boxes that you think about: the Box of Work, the Box of Money, the Box of Sex, and possibly, the Box of a Hobby. These are the natural go-to subjects in the minds of most men. A man does not frequently think about the non-negotiables his wife wants and needs. Therefore, a husband has to be *intentional* about creating a new box for his shelf, the Box of Wife. *Intentionally* you must take this box off the shelf—which contains the eleven non-negotiable tenets in *Husband School*—and be proactive in giving these nutrients to your garden. Otherwise, you will continue to repeatedly take only your four favorite boxes off your shelf. Your *willingness* to take the Box of Wife off your shelf is a *decision*, not necessarily a *desire*. Since wives are engineered to be responders, your willingness to take the Box of Wife off your shelf makes you the Game Changer in marriage."

Tomorrow is Thanksgiving, and I'm hoping to take the Box of Football off the shelf as much as possible.

"As I have repeatedly said, a husband is basically satisfied in his marriage if he gets enough sex, and his wife does not bring too much emotional turmoil into the relationship. But in contrast, a wife has many conditions that she wants met before she is satisfied. In fact, a wife's satisfaction is predicated to a large degree upon her husband's willingness to meet her many needs and desires."

Many is an understatement, but I've made peace with that.

"As we've said, it's difficult for a husband to treat his wife in a manner he finds unnecessary or inconvenient. But when a husband chooses *against* his natural inclinations and instead, unselfishly gives his wife these eleven non-negotiable secrets, he will discover that she easily responds with good humor, brightness, and a desire to please him."

I already see the truth of this principle playing out.

"Let me remind you that for centuries, men have wanted devotion and affection from their wives without first giving her these eleven non-negotiable principles. It is like demanding that a garden be grand with little or no care. Or it is like asking a car to run well without gasoline or regular maintenance. These are the secret keys to a vibrant marriage, and no matter how smart, rich, shrewd, or powerful you are, you will not win your wife's heart without giving your garden these eleven nutrients."

As much as I hate to admit it, I know he's right.

"However, if you do choose to give your wife these eleven precepts, you will see a woman *bloom right before your eyes*. But a husband must first decide if he's willing to pay the price. That's why husbands are the Game Changers and why husbands primarily determine the quality of the marriage. Wives respond to this treatment,[58] just like a garden responds to sunlight, good soil, water, and consistent care. You are the gardener. Your care to a large degree determines the richness of your garden."

The truth of what he is saying is again pressing on my chest.

---

58. Both spouses respond to how the other spouse treats them, but the wives we have worked with seem especially predisposed to do so.

"When a wife consistently receives the eleven non-negotiable tenets from her husband, she feels cherished, loved, and safe. And when she feels cherished, loved, and safe, she will work to make you happy."

I would click the "Like" button if I was on social media.

"All of life is deeper and richer for any man when he experiences it with a warm and devoted wife," he says. "But again, having a happy, warm, and devoted wife has a high price."

These last few weeks have turned my whole thinking about marriage upside down. As unpleasant as the thought is of giving all these nutrients to my garden, I know that to have a great marriage, there is really no other choice.

"I am not denying that *Husband School* is a large amount of work," he continues, "but men expect to work hard to succeed in their calling or hobby. But on the one relationship that determines the overwhelming part of their domestic happiness, they do not show a similar work ethic. When a man repeatedly loves his wife *as he loves himself,* one day he will realize his marriage is like a beautiful, flowery meadow, almost blissful."

I'm not there yet, but with the trajectory we're on, I can see how one day that might be the case.

"Many men give their wives these eleven non-negotiable principles because they want their wife *to give back to them.* But that is merely manipulation, Young Jason. In contrast, your motivation for loving Christina in this manner should be because you want to please the Creator. I cannot fix your heart, Young Jason. Only when you are in prayer and in the Creator's Word will you renew your mind and change your heart."

I admit it. I have previously focused on *giving to get.* But now I see that my prior thinking was a manipulative mindset. Finally, I am ready to love Christina with my motivation being to please the Creator. It's a subtle, but huge, change.

"I am leaving now," he says, "but you possess the knowledge to have one of the most incredible marriages on earth. Just remember, as I've said earlier, the number one quality a wife desires in her husband is *trustworthiness*.[59] Be sure you have impeccable integrity in all areas."

If trustworthiness is so important, why didn't the Genie devote one of the eleven non-negotiables to that? Thinking about that, though, I think I know the answer. Any rational human being knows that *one expects impeccable integrity from their spouse, so of course, Christina expects it from me*.[60] The Genie assumed I didn't need a lesson on trustworthiness. But thinking about my failure to tell Christina about Delaney, my failure to tell Christina about buying golf clubs, as well as my failure to be trustworthy to show up on time at Isabella's dance program, I think maybe I could have used a twelfth non-negotiable principle. Trustworthiness, I also realize, is the number one quality I expect from Christina.

"My work is done," he continues. "Therefore, please find someone else who has a problem and give the lantern to him." For the last time, the Genie twirls into his hurricane-looking swirl of smoke and reenters the Aladdin-looking lantern.

Although I have been repeatedly annoyed by the rantings and railings of the old guy, I know that my marriage will never be the same.

Arriving home, Christina announces she has made my favorite meal, Paleo pizza. Christina begins listing all the steps she took to make the cauliflower crust and the homemade sauce. And although cooking is not exactly my favorite topic, I know wives love husbands to listen attentively to all of their topics (Deep Conversation), so I perch on one of the kitchen bar stools and listen intently, Hitting the Ping Pong Ball Back.

At dinner, I tell Christina it may be her best pizza ever while I lift up her hand to kiss it (Admiration and Nonsexual Touching).

During dinner, the kids tell me about their day at school, and after dinner, I take turns throwing each of them in the air, to their repeated

---

59. Not only are you to be trustworthy with other women, your words, and your money, but you are also to be trustworthy to *show up* and do what you say you will do. Don't make promises or plans that you don't keep.

60. "So in everything, do to others what you would have them do to you, for this sums up the Law and the Prophets" (Matt. 7:12).

squeals of delight (rocking Fatherhood). Depositing multiple nutrients like this into my garden is now a daily event.

The children are excused to go play, and while carrying dishes to the sink (Household Help), I tell Christina everything in detail about my meeting with Kevin White. As the kids meander back to the table to get apple slices for dessert, Christina announces, "You kids have a very smart daddy!"

Isabella raises her apple slice high, like it's a flag, and chirps, "We have the best daddy ever!"

Mason also raises his apple slice high in the air, mimicking his older sister, chiming in, "Best! Best!" The baby, Samantha, hits her spoon on her high-chair tray, as if to signify that she agrees too. Looking at Christina's smile, I am filled with a satisfaction and fulfillment that I rarely remember feeling. I kiss the top of her head (more Nonsexual Touching), and I can see by her expression she likes it.

After I help put the kids to bed (rocking Fatherhood again), Christina tells me she is going to take a bath. No one says anything else, but we both know it is Wednesday, a scheduled night (yippee!). Christina walks out in a short pink nightgown, towel drying her hair.

"Christina, I've been thinking about how much you want another baby," I say. "I've realized my objection is the financial pressure I would feel, since you also want the kids to go to private school. What if we had a fourth child and you homeschooled, or we moved to a neighborhood that had a good public school if we don't have the finances for private education?"

With Kevin White's help, I think I'll be okay with finances, but I'm not sure, of course, so I want to get this issue clear before we get pregnant again.

That began a forty-five minute discussion of how she would love to homeschool for the first few years, and of course, she would consider moving to a better school district if our income couldn't handle private education.

"Jason, I want you to know how happy I am in our marriage. You have become the nicest and best husband I've ever seen. I just want to tell you how loved and cherished I feel, and that it gives me a deep happiness. I've never been happier in my whole life."

Stunned, I stop and look at this creature, this creature who used to constantly criticize me, who would rarely support me, and who even less frequently agreed to have sex. And now, she's telling me that I'm the best husband ever and that she has never been happier. And the best part, the very best part, is that we're getting ready to have sex. Wow. My garden is blooming.

"I love you, Christina," I say. And I mean it. Not only do I feel love for her, but I am determined to treat her in a manner that will please the Creator.

Smiling as she slips into bed, she replies, "I love you, too, Jason."

Who could ever believe that our marriage would absolutely flip like it's done in the last few weeks? The Genie's eleven non-negotiable lessons have been agonizing, but they worked. They absolutely worked! Learning that women want something totally different from men, I now give Christina things that are, in my estimation, unnecessary and inconvenient. This is definitely how to love a woman in a language she can hear.

Life will not always be perfect, but my marriage is certainly headed in a fabulous, wonderful direction.

Now, it's time to turn off the lights and enjoy my sweet wife.

SUMMARY OF CONCLUSION

Understand That Husbands—Not Wives— Are the Game Changers in Marriage

Do...

. . . realize that you, the husband, largely determine the quality of your marriage because your tendency is to think about work, sex, money, not your wife. You must choose to take the Box of Wife off the shelf.

. . . realize that you must treat your wife in a manner that you often find unnecessary and inconvenient.

. . . remember that women are responders, and when given the eleven nonnegotiable principles, they respond with good humor, brightness, and a desire to please.

. . . realize there is a price to pay for having a fabulous marriage. Men expect to work hard to excel in their calling or hobby, but for the one relationship that largely determines their domestic happiness, they expect it to grow lavishly by itself.

Don't...

. . . expect devotion and affection from your wife without first giving her the eleven tenets. That's like asking a garden to be grand with little or no care.

. . . forget that the single most important quality in your wife's mind is your trustworthiness.

The End

A Compilation of All Summaries in *Husband School*

Summary of Introduction:
Understand That You Are the Gardener

Do...

> . . . know that marriage is not an unpredictable, chaotic situation. You can learn the patterns and skills to promote harmony, friendship, and affection.

> . . . know that when a woman consistently receives the eleven *Husband School* tenets, she will turn to you and be interested in your happiness because women are responders.

> . . . view yourself as the gardener who must supply what his garden needs. A woman does not have the same needs you have.

> . . . know there are rules how you must treat your wife if you want her to be happy in your marriage.

Don't...

> . . . expect your garden to bloom without much attention and care.

> . . . assume that the mind of a woman is unknowable. The mind of a woman has been dissected, analyzed, and categorized. It is not impossible or difficult to understand.

Summary of Lesson 1:
Understand Your Wife's Desire for Deep Conversation

Do...

> . . . realize that not having Deep Conversation with your wife feels like indifference and neglect to her.

> . . . realize that a woman's soul aches for a husband who will give her World Class Listening and who will Hit the Ping Pong Ball Back.

> . . . know that your wife is delighted when you Initiate Conversations of Significance.

> . . . know that your wife wants to be known, explored, and understood by you.

> . . . take the Shield Off Your Heart, and share your hopes, dreams, regrets, and goals.

Don't...

> . . . treat her as she deserves. Instead, give your garden what it needs.

> . . . assume your wife wants sex like you do, but realize most wives want talk (Emotional Release) to the extent that you want sex (Sexual Release).

Summary of Lesson 2:
Understand Your Wife's Desire for
Admiration and Appreciation

Do...

> ... intentionally think about your wife's virtues, gifts, and abilities, and then comment on them (Admiration).

> ... realize that your wife wants to be reminded *daily* about her positive qualities, actions, and talents.

> ... realize that criticism is the opposite of Admiration.

> ... notice what benefits you receive from your wife and comment on them daily (Appreciation).

Don't...

> ... admire or brag on other women.

> ... think that if you're faithful, dutiful, and a good provider, then you are free from giving your wife this non-negotiable tenet.

Summary of Lesson 3:
Understand How Your Wife Feels about the Big Five

Do...

    . . . realize that a wife often measures how much you care about her by how well you show up for her on the Big Five.

    . . . make each of the Big Five an event.

    . . . realize that many women have a hard time asking for things, so you have to suggest ideas.

    . . . realize that each woman has a playbook in her heart for how she wants to celebrate the Big Five, and you have to extract it.

    . . . realize that she expects the Big Five, so if you really want to rock it, get her a SUG (Surprise and Unexpected Gift).

Don't...

    . . . discount or ignore this lesson because you feel radically different about it.

    . . . assume you know what she wants without first checking it out.

    . . . wait until the last minute to make plans to celebrate the Big Five.

Summary of Lesson 4:
Understand Your Wife's Perspective on Sex

Do...

. . . realize that most men have a higher appetite for sex than women.

. . . realize that your wife only wants to have sex with you if she feels that, in her opinion, you have been "a good husband." (Although this is incorrect thinking on women's part, this is how they often feel.)

. . . realize that your wife must feel your honest attempt to love, cherish, and know her if you want her to be a willing and engaged sex partner.

. . . realize that wives are highly offended if you show any interest in other women.

. . . realize that a woman's sex organ is her brain. A lifestyle of attention, making her feel beautiful, desirable, important, and wanted, is the foreplay she desires.

. . . consider scheduling if you and your wife desire different amounts of sex, or if you are very busy and need to protect your intimate time together.

. . . realize that women adore Nonsexual Touching at times when you aren't trying to get sex.

Don't...

. . . expect your wife to be turned on by your nakedness, from being nibbled on the neck, or by having her sex organs groped.

. . . expect to naturally know how to sexually stimulate and satisfy your wife.

. . . think porn is harmless; it's devastating to your marriage and repugnant to the Lord.

Summary of Lesson 5:
Understand How Your Wife Feels
about Managing the Household

Do...

> . . . realize that women become upset when they have little or no discretionary time, but you have plenty.

> . . . realize that if your wife feels overwhelmed with the responsibilities of the household, she expects you to help her solve this problem, either by helping her yourself or hiring some help, or figuring out any another solution.

> . . . consider offering to help her with household tasks that you don't mind doing.

> . . . consider cutting back on other expenses to hire household help for her.

> . . . have a conversation with her to see how she feels about the management of the household.

Don't...

> . . . decide that household tasks are traditional female work and refuse to help.

Summary of Lesson 6:
Understand How Money
Management Affects Your Wife

Do...

> ... realize that the primary breadwinner, when it is the husband, has a tendency to think his opinions about spending, saving, investing, and giving are more important than his wife's.

> ... realize that when an *imbalance of power* occurs (i.e., when one spouse's opinions matter more than the other's), the weaker spouse resents the one with power.

> ... realize that using a software program like Quicken or Microsoft Money, and looking at black-and-white numbers on a computer screen together, helps a couple devise a joint money strategy.

> ... realize that the more both spouses know about the subject of their finances, the less conflict there will be.

> ... realize that most women always have—and most women always will—expect men to shoulder and bear the couple's finances.

> ... get rid of debt and then propose to save.

Don't...

> ... discount a woman's love of beauty just because it's not important to you.

> ... let your wife lose respect for you by not adequately providing.

> ... make large purchases without the wholehearted consent of the other.

Summary of Lesson 7:
Understand How Your Wife Feels
about Your Role as a Father

Do...

... realize that your fathering is one of the most important gifts you give your wife.

... realize that the bond between you and your children affects their social, psychological, and even physical development.

... realize that children feel loved by their father according to the amount of time their father spends with them.

... express warmth and affection to your children: touch, hold, and kiss them.

... learn to apologize and ask forgiveness.

... find a father who loves his children well, and spend time watching how he does it.

... realize that the time a father spends with his children radically changes the direction of their lives.

Don't...

... be jealous of your wife's attention to the children. In contrast, assist her in providing everything the children need to function well.

... react inappropriately to a child's disobedience or misconduct. Instead, use self-control with your voice and especially, your hands. A father's anger crushes a child's spirit.

... neglect children who are difficult. They are the ones who need your attention the most.

Summary of Lesson 8:
Understand Your Wife's Desire
for Affection and Romance

Do...

... realize that although most men do not care about Affection and Romance, women never outgrow their desire for it.

... give tender words daily.

... realize that if you fail to give your wife Affection and Romance, she will want it from other men.

... give your wife plenty of Nonsexual Touching.

... look into her eyes and smile.

Don't...

... give Affection and Romance merely when you have a sexual urge, but try to give it at other times.

... think your wife is like the radical fringe who wants to open her own doors.

... neglect giving your wife Affection and Romance just because the hormones driving it are gone. Choose to give it to her.

Summary of Lesson 9:
Understand the Leadership Style Your Wife Needs

Do...

. . . remember that a Sacrificial/Servant Leadership style husband cares about his wife's welfare as much as his own.

. . . realize that a wife who is well loved over time will not have as much difficulty submitting to his leadership.

. . . earn the right to lead by humbly serving your wife.

. . . remember that wise leaders overlook, forgive, don't keep a record of wrongs, and return a blessing for insult.

. . . remember that since you're the leader, you go first.

Don't...

. . . expect your wife to submit just because of your position of head, without first loving her well.

. . . be inconsiderate of or neglect your wife's dreams, hopes, goals, and comfort.

Summary of Lesson 10: Understand How Anger and Harsh Words Affect Your Wife

Do...

. . . realize your wife is easily wounded by your anger and harsh words.

. . . remember that self-control—not giving in to your natural inclinations—is always the virtue.

. . . accept your wife's weakness set.

. . . enforce the Forty-eight Hour Rule when you are upset with your wife.

. . . learn how to ask forgiveness.

. . . aim for a twenty-five to one ratio of positive to negative comments with your wife.

Don't...

. . . use harshness, disrespect, or increased volume when talking to your wife.

Summary of Lesson 11:
Understand Your Wife's Desire for the One Thing

Do...

. . . realize that you have to acknowledge your wife's One Thing, by either trying to resolve or negotiate the issue.

Don't...

. . . belittle, talk disrespectfully to her, be annoyed, impatient, or condescending over the One Thing.

. . . ignore her One Thing.

Summary of Conclusion:
Understand That Husbands—Not Wives—
Are the Game Changers in Marriage

Do...

... realize that you, the husband, largely determine the quality of your marriage.

... realize that because your tendency is to think mainly about work, sex, money (and not your wife), you must choose to take the Box of Wife off the shelf.

... realize that you must treat your wife in a manner that you often find unnecessary and inconvenient.

... remember that women are responders, and when given the eleven non-negotiable principles, respond with good humor, brightness, and a desire to please.

... realize there is a price to pay for having a fabulous marriage. Men expect to work hard to succeed in their calling or hobby, but for the one relationship that largely determines their domestic happiness, they expect it to grow lavishly by itself.

Don't...

... expect devotion and affection from your wife without first giving her the eleven tenets. That's like asking a garden to be grand with little or no care.

... forget that the single most important quality in your wife's mind is your trustworthiness.

Twelve-Week
Group Discussion Guide

Note to facilitator and group members: Groups of four to ten men seem to work best. Plan forty-five minutes to an hour each week to discuss the questions. Each group member should try to not talk more than his share, but likewise, he should try to contribute to the discussion each week. In addition, each member should pretend his wife is listening when he talks and be careful not to disrespect her in any way. If there are no responses to a question, just go to the next one.

Week 1

Before the first meeting, read Introduction, Understand That You Are the Gardener.

1. Was there anything new to you in the way women want to be loved? Explain.

2. Have you thought the mind of a woman was an endless pit of knots and tangles? Was it surprising to you that learning the mind of a woman is merely a minor learning project? Were you surprised to learn that marriage is not an unpredictable, chaotic situation, but rather there are patterns and behaviors that produce discord and conflict just as there are patterns and skills that produce harmony? Explain.

3. Are you a husband like the Genie describes, in that what you believe is love is bringing home your paycheck, having sex, and sharing activities together (without discussing the relationship)? Describe what you think.

4. How do you react to the statement that women are responders and that when your garden is given the right nutrients, she produces a fruitful crop?

5. How do you react to the Genie's statement that Christina is not hysterical and mentally unbalanced but merely feels frustrated because she does not feel understood and cherished?

6. How do you feel about the Genie's statement that when women are given "the proper amount of sunlight and nutrients, they bloom every time"?

7. After men get married, they often feel that their garden should grow lush by itself, instead of realizing that the work to have a bountiful garden has just begun. How do you feel about that statement?

8. Do you agree that men think about 30 percent work, 30 percent money, and 30 percent sex? Do you see the problem that only 10 percent is left for everything else? Do you see how infrequently you think about your wife and understand that if you love her according to your natural inclinations, she will not be well loved? Explain.

9. The Genie gave Jason a list of what he wanted from the marriage: praise, appreciation, respect, letting him lead, assistance, adaptation, attractiveness, warmth, affection, fun, a companion for activities, a great listener, a good cook, a good mother, a good housekeeper, and an exciting sex partner. Did he miss anything? (What about a spiritual challenge? What about intellectual stimulation? Do you care about any of these virtues? What others?)

10. The Genie said that a husband's normal tendency is to focus on what he is *not* being given, such as respect, credit, praise, appreciation, sex, and a willingness to adapt and follow. How do you feel about laying down these desires and first learning to meet your wife's needs before you ask her to meet yours? Explain.

11. The minds of women have been dissected, analyzed, and categorized. What she wants is not impossible to discover or understand. The challenge is for a man to give his wife something he thinks is unnecessary and inconvenient. How do you react to this statement?

12. In order to fully enjoy and experience life, men desire a warm relationship with a woman with whom to share life. However, there are rules written in the DNA of women of how they want to be treated by their husbands. Are you willing to concede to what has been true for centuries? Explain your thoughts.

Week 2

Before the meeting, read Lesson 1, Understand Your Wife's Desire for Deep Conversation.

1. Did you know that a woman wants Emotional Release, gained by Deep Conversation, to the extent that you want Sexual Release? Were you aware that not having Deep Conversation with your wife feels like neglect and indifference to her? Explain.

2. Evaluate your World Class Listening skill set. How well do you think you do? Evaluate your skill of Hitting the Ping Pong Ball Back. How could you improve?

3. When Jason said that Christina's topics were boring, the Genie told him to quit wasting time and energy thinking about that because this is the woman he was given to love. How do you respond to that?

4. In *Wife School*, the Genie teaches women that willingness is the first step in sex, not desire. In *Husband School*, the Genie teaches men that willingness is the first step in giving Christina World Class Listening, not desire. What thoughts do you have about this?

5. The Genie says that husbands are to Initiate Conversations of Significance because no wife is richly satisfied without sharing deep topics, such as her fears and dreams. How well do you do at Initiating Conversations of Significance? What questions stir your wife's desire to share deeply?

6. The Genie says that no wife deserves being treated this well, but that regardless, it's your duty and responsibility to love your wife in a language she can hear. What are your thoughts in response to that statement?

7. The Genie said that because Christina does not feel known, explored, and understood by Jason, she does not want to be affectionate, admiring, or have frequent sex. How do you feel about going first and giving your wife what she needs (but doesn't necessarily deserve?)

8. Taking the Shield Off Your Heart is difficult for many men, as they do not frequently think about deep topics, such as their hopes, dreams, regrets, and goals. How are you with Taking the Shield Off Your Heart and sharing with your wife? Explain.

9. Is twenty to thirty minutes a day a realistic goal for you to give your wife Deep Conversation? Explain.

Week 3

Before the meeting, read Lesson 2, Understand Your Wife's Desire for Admiration and Appreciation.

1. Have you had the mindset that giving people too much Appreciation and Admiration "keeps them in their place" or "keeps them from getting a big head"? Explain.

2. Have you made peace with the fact that you give your wife what she needs and wants, so she can function at a higher level versus what she deserves? Explain.

3. Intentionally thinking about your wife's virtues, gifts, abilities, and then commenting on them, is *not* the normal habit of most husbands. How could you grow this habit?

4. Does giving your wife *daily* Admiration and Appreciation seem like overkill to you? What are your thoughts?

5. Have you realized that bragging on other women is diametrically opposed to giving your wife Admiration? Did you know that the opposite of Admiration is criticism? Explain your thinking.

6. Share with the group some things you appreciate about your wife. Then go home tonight, and tell your wife what you told the group.

7. Did you realize what huge power you have over your wife's self-esteem? Did you previously realize what constant reassurance she needs about her beauty, desirability, and gifts? Explain your thoughts.

Week 4

Before the meeting, read Lesson 3, Understand How Your Wife Feels about the Big Five.

1. Men feel radically different than women about the Big Five. What has been your previous mindset about celebrating the Big Five?

2. Does it seem logical to you that women measure how much people care about them by how others show up for them on their special days, the Big Five? Do you feel like the list of items that the Genie gives Jason (the wrapped present, the flowers, the mushy card, to be taken out to dinner) are overkill? Explain.

3. The Genie tells Jason that many women have a hard time asking for things, so therefore, you have to suggest things. Are you willing to do this? Explain.

4. Many men feel very inadequate about celebrating a wife's special days. What ideas from this chapter were helpful to you?

5. What is your reaction to the concept of SUGs, Surprise and Unexpected Gifts? Explain.

6. Know that if you have a conversation with your wife about the Big Five, she will probably *not* tell you to roll out the red carpet for her. But deep in her heart, she wants this kind of attention. You do not have to spend a lot of money, but you do have to give a lot of attention. What is your reaction to this?

7. Men are burdened with the task of extracting how a woman feels. But if you do not celebrate the Big Five in a specific manner she desires, she will feel unloved and unknown. What is your reaction to this?

8. Jason says his previous mindset is being dismantled. Since he's the man, he thought she was the one to be his personal assistant. Yet the

Genie continually asks Jason to not be concerned with how Christina is treating him, but to focus on how he treats her. What are your thoughts with this paradigm shift?

Week 5

Before the meeting, read Lesson 4, Understand Your Wife's Perspective about Sex.

This is a particularly private lesson, so please do not share anything negative about your wife. This lesson is geared to the traditional gender model in which men desire sex more than women (about 80 percent of marriages). If you are in the 20 percent of marriages where your wife has a higher sex drive than you, have your wife read chapter 32 in *Wife School*. Today's discussion is geared toward the 80 percent.

1. Many men feel there is something wrong with their wife's sexual desire, thinking that most women are like the women in the movies, ready and excited on a moment's notice to have sex. But the reality is that men usually have a much higher appetite for sex than their wives. Have you been deceived by the culture's TV and movies? Explain.

2. Are you angry at the thought that your wife only wants to have sex when she feels like you deserve it? Explain.

3. Did you realize that when wives feel threatened in any way by other women, they do not want to have sex? Did you previously know how highly offensive it is to your wife when you are excited by another woman?

4. What do you think about the statement that to a wife, trustworthiness is the single most important quality in a husband?

5. Did you previously think that women are stimulated by the sight of a man's naked body in the same way that you are stimulated by a woman's naked body? Of course, you realize that your sex organ is six inches below your waist, but did you realize her sex organ is her brain? Explain.

6. What do you think about the way the Genie described the foreplay that your wife wants, that is, that she wants you to flirt with her, tease her, notice her, be interested in her, and compliment her? The Genie said that foreplay to your wife is the daily attention you give her to make her feel beautiful, desired, wanted, and admired. What is your reaction to that?

7. What are your thoughts about how many wives want to bathe before they have sex and for you to have a bath, brush your teeth, etc,?

8. The Genie said that to women, sex is the culmination of a great relationship, of trusting you, of having much conversation, and of feeling loved, cherished, and known. What is your reaction to this?

9. Men come with software for eating, sleeping, and ejaculating, but not lovemaking. Comment on this statement.

10. Does the concept of scheduling sex make you angry? Explain.

11. What are your thoughts about Nonsexual Touching? Explain.

12. The Genie said that men were never created to see women's unclothed bodies before marriage. Is this an outrageous thought to you, in light of today's culture? Explain.

13. Porn is rampant but is absolutely devastating to marriage. Read the footnote at the end of Lesson 4 on porn. What are your comments?

Week 6

Before the meeting, read Lesson 5, Understand How Your Wife Feels about Managing the Household.

1. To many women, managing the household is a burden. How does your wife feel about household tasks?

2. Do you feel that managing the household is a female role? What is your reaction to the list the Genie gave Jason, Common Household Tasks?

3. With which household jobs could you offer help?

4. How important is negotiating the household workload to your wife? Explain.

5. Would you consider driving an older car, living in a smaller house, or not going out as often in order to get your wife some household help? Explain.

6. How did you react to the Genie's statement that if you relax while your wife is overworked and feels burdened with the household, then she will interpret this as you not caring about her?

Week 7

Before the meeting, read Lesson 6, Understand How Money Management Affects Your Wife.

1. The norm in marriages is that the primary breadwinner makes the decisions. What is your opinion about this?

2. The Genie says the average man assumes that being in charge means giving orders that benefit himself. But a man who understands true headship considers his wife's desires, needs, and opinions equal with his own. Respond to this thought.

3. An imbalance of power results when one spouse's opinions matter more than the other spouse's, resulting in the weaker spouse resenting the one in power. Is this something you've noticed? Explain.

4. The Genie recommends getting computer software and looking at black and white numbers on a screen. What do you think about a budget?

5. Sharing money decisions is very difficult for many men. How do you feel about this?

6. What is your reaction to a woman's love of beauty and allowing for some of it in the budget?

7. When the main breadwinner is the wife, traditional female roles must be at least somewhat embraced by the husband (childcare, cooking, housework, errands, etc.). This is often a problem because men usually don't have an antenna for that kind of work. What are your thoughts on this subject?

8. The Genie says that full disclosure of all income, as well as all expenditures, is necessary because trust and honesty are the foundations of any relationship. Respond to this.

Week 8

Before the meeting, read Lesson 7, Understand How Your Wife Feels about Your Role as a Father.

1. Were you previously aware of how your involvement with your children affected your wife's feelings toward you? Does your wife rate your fathering as one of the most important gifts you give her? Explain.

2. Were you previously aware that a woman does not separate her child's well-being from her own? Explain.

3. It is easy for some men to be jealous of their wife's attention to the children, when they do not understand the wife's passionate love for them. How do you feel about this?

4. Did you previously know that the bond between a father and his child affects the child's social behavior, psychological well-being, and even the development of his brain? How do you feel about that?

5. Children feel loved by their father according to the amount of time the father spends with them. What is your reaction to this statement?

6. Although many fathers model courage, risk-taking, and industry well to their offspring, they stumble in demonstrating affection and kindness. What is your tendency with your children?

7. A father's reaction to his child's disobedience or misconduct is as important as anything else the father does with the child. It is critical that the father learns to control his voice and his hands. Discuss the self-control and patience needed to be a good father.

8. You will make mistakes with your children. Are you able to apologize and ask forgiveness?

9. Children who are difficult to love are the ones who need it the most. You must guard against your natural inclination to give what is easy

instead of your responsibility to give what your children need. Respond to this statement and the fact that work and hobbies often provide more immediate satisfaction than spending time with your children.

Week 9

Before the meeting, read Lesson 8, Understand Your Wife's Desire for Affection and Romance.

1. Admiration is expressing what a wife does well. Appreciation is letting your wife know the benefits she brings to your life. *Affection* and *romance* are words expressing your positive feelings toward her. Does it seem like expressing all these words to your wife is overdoing it? Explain.

2. Does your wife like romantic movies or books? What does this say about her love of romance?

3. Do you mainly give Affection and Romance when you have a sexual urge? Do you understand why that doesn't count in a woman's mind since you are trying to get something?

4. Since you mainly think about work, money, and sex, it is often difficult to give your wife a steady stream of tender words. Explain how you feel about this.

5. How do you feel about giving your wife Good Manners? Is your wife delighted when you treat her with tenderness?

6. Many men only like Sexual Touching. But women mainly like Non-sexual Touching. What are your thoughts on this?

7. If you do not fill your wife's tank with repeated deposits of Affection and Romance, she will desire this attention from other men. Although this is wrong, this is how many women feel. Describe how this makes you feel.

8. Do you still have regular, sustained romantic eye contact with your wife? Discuss.

Week 10

Before the meeting, read Lesson 9, Understand the Leadership Style Your Wife Needs.

1. A husband with the commander style thinks that because he is the head of the marriage, and his wife should comply with his orders. He also thinks his happiness, goals, and concerns are more important than his wife's. Comment on this.

2. Ephesians 5:28 says a husband is to love his wife as his own body. Ephesians 5:25 says a husband is to love his wife as Christ loved the church, and gave himself up for her. Considering the analogy of marriage being a picture of Jesus and the church, we can deduce from Romans 5:8 ("while we were still sinners, Christ died for us"), that a man should love his wife without her first being deserving of it. These are very strong statements. Respond to these thoughts.

3. Have you previously understood that a woman being created for the man meant that his wife would be his completer, his companion, and his helper in fulfilling his call to be fruitful, multiply, and subdue the earth? Or did you previously think that was she was merely given to man for his increased comfort and convenience? Explain.

4. When two people marry, they become one, according to Mark 10:8. Taking care of your wife is taking care of yourself. How do you feel about this?

5. The Passive Leadership style chooses the path of least resistance and let's his wife run the family, rather than enter the chaos of family life. Passive Leadership husbands want to avoid conflict, although this style of inattention and neglect make a wife feel unloved. What are your thoughts on Passive Leadership?

6. The husband who has a Sacrificial/Servant style of Leadership considers the interests of his wife as important as his own. Discuss how you could grow in this area.

7. A woman who is well loved over time will not have as much difficulty submitting to her husband's leadership. Discuss the implications this

statement has concerning your wife's resistance to your leadership.

8. A husband does not demand that his wife follow him because he holds the position and title of head, but rather, he earns the right to lead and influence by humbly serving his wife. What does this mean to your marriage?

9. Your wife knows when her dreams, hopes, and goals are equal in your mind with hers and likewise, she knows when you see her as a mere aid to assist you in your journey. Comment on how you could improve this area with your wife.

10. Wise leaders lead by doing what is right, by overlooking, by forgiving, by not keeping a record of wrongs, and returning a blessing for insult. Comment on how you're doing in this area.

Week 11

Before the meeting, read Lesson 10, Understand How Anger and Harsh Words Affect Your Wife

1. Have you previously realized that your wife has a sensitivity to your remarks like a person with a sunburn has a sensitivity to a bump? Explain.

2. Although the natural inclination is to raise your voice and use a strong tone when you are upset, mature people can learn to communicate without using harshness, disrespect, or volume. Comment on this truth.

3. Often, husbands think they get to let down at home since they have been using self-control all day at work. However, saying uncontrolled and improper words to your wife can have disastrous consequences. What are some thoughts about this?

4. You were attracted to and married a woman with an opposite personality. But now those different traits are the very things that annoy you about your wife. Learning to accept your wife's weakness set is part of every marriage. What is your reaction to this?

5. Do you think the Forty-eight Hour Rule could help you eliminate firing off critical remarks in the passion of the moment? Explain.

6. Men are slow to ask forgiveness, hoping that the conflict will fade away. But conflict accumulates—unless one apologizes. Comment on this truth.

7. Thriving interpersonal relationships are comprised of a ratio of high positive deposits to low negative deposits. What kind of ratio is going on in your marriage? Discuss.

Week 12

Before the meeting, read Lesson 11, Understand Your Wife's Desire for the One Thing and Conclusion, Understand That Husbands—Not Wives—Are the Game Changers in Marriage.

1. Every woman will have the One Thing she wants from you. It's the thing she asks you for all the time, the thing you don't want to give. How do you feel about your wife's One Thing?

2. The norm is for most husbands to ignore their wife's One Thing, instead of discussing it, negotiating it, or moving toward her with problem solving. What is your tendency toward your wife's One Thing?

3. Although wives expect to accommodate their husbands all the time, husbands do not want to accommodate their wives very often. How do you feel about this?

4. Although you are annoyed by the topic of your wife's One Thing, you must move toward her in some way in this area. How do you feel about this?

Questions from conclusion:

5. The Genie told Jason he's the Game Changer in his marriage. Your wife is a garden, and you are the gardener. If you give her the care and attention she needs, she will respond with fruitfulness. Comment on this idea.

6. The husband is the Game Changer because he has to choose against his natural inclinations and instead, give his wife what he thinks is unnecessary and inconvenient in order to make her happy. Respond to this truth.

7. A husband primarily determines the quality of the marriage because he decides if he's willing to pay the price and love his wife in a language that she can hear. How do you feel about this?

8. Now that you understand what a woman wants and needs, what will be some easy changes for you to make to improve your marriage? What will be the difficult choices or changes for you to make? Discuss.

About the Authors

David Gordon is a board-certified trial attorney but is frequently sought out for his wise and godly counsel in business as well as interpersonal relationships. His wife, Julie, has a master's degree in Marriage and Family Counseling and has also written *Wife School, Where Women Learn the Secrets of Making Husbands Happy, Skinny School, Where Women Learn the Secrets to Finally Get Thin Forever, and Happy School, Where Women Learn the Secrets to Overcome Discouragement and Worry.*

Julie and David have been married for thirty-three years, but not all of those years have been blissful (e.g., rearing six children, starting a business from scratch during midlife, health issues, and the like). However, Julie and David would both say that the friendship, comfort, companionship, and faithfulness of the other is near the top of what makes life fulfilling.

Living in Memphis, David and Julie have begun a new venture together, grandparenting (which is a whole lot easier than parenting!).

You can learn about other books and events at **JulieNGordon.com**. David and Julie can be contacted at **HusbandSchool@gmail.com**.

www.ingramcontent.com/pod-product-compliance
Lightning Source LLC
Chambersburg PA
CBHW051421090426
42737CB00014B/2772